MILK AND COOKIES

Maggie Mueller

16, November
2019

To Connie ~

I hope you enjoy
reading all of our
antics!

Happy Reading!!

Maggie Mueller

This book is dedicated to Alex, Jasmine, Devon, Chloe and Mikeala, my beautiful grandchildren. Their zest for fun and unconditional love has inspired me to put pieces of their lives on paper so
I will never forget;
to my Spiritual family for their love
and support.
To my biological family for giving me
endless material.
And to my husband Dave, who has given me
guidance and patience.
Mary Zastudil, thanks for always having
time to answer my unending questions,
And to my mom who always believes in me.

But most of all to my Inspiration, my Lord, Jesus, who I believe took my hands and made them instruments for His words.
He gives me life, love and grace and
I am blessed.

Preface

Welcome to my kitchen table. It is a place where friends and family gather together and talk over life and times. All subjects are up for grabs when we meet there and we always share something fun to eat.

Our home isn't so unusual. Most families gather to laugh and play and grow. The older folks tell stories about their childhood as the younger ones sit and listen while munching on some milk and cookies.

The stories are never forgotten and are retold through the generations, perhaps embellished on but treasured tales none the less. And even though we know the punch line, we laugh. Some of the tales are sad and we cry, and some are discussion causing and thought provoking.

Each story telling time helps to bind us together tightly with love and caring. We all embrace each other and hold tight to our heritage.

The stories in this book are some of the memories I have held near to my heart. All of them are precious to me and bring back fond memories as I read them. I want to share them with you. I hope they bring as much delight to you as you read them as they did for me when I wrote them.

So pull up a chair and I'll set out a plate of Milk and Cookies for us to share.

Maggie Mueller

Contents

January

February

March

April

May

June

July

August

September

October

November

December

January

Family

Family, what a strange word. There are nine different meanings for it in the dictionary. The first is obvious, parents and their children.

But what really constitutes a family? Do you have to be biologically connected to be a family? Of course not, being a family means a gathering of people (or things) that relate to each other. We can have biological family members who don't relate to us in belief systems, lifestyles or thought processes. But on the other hand, we can have friends, people unrelated by blood, be our closest family.

Okay you say, what's my point?

We spent the holidays in Florida. Yeah, suffering for Jesus. But in a sense, we really were. Although we were with our children and their families, we felt a detachment, kind of out of place. It almost felt as if we were on Mars. The little nucleus of people in our clan felt strangely separated from the rest of the people in the area where we were staying. I didn't understand it. Here I was with my children, my grandgirls and my husband and I wasn't content.

Now don't get me wrong, there is nothing I would rather do than to play with my little girls who are precious gifts from God; Alex with her little red curls dancing with every step and Jasmine with her quiet fawn eyes taking in everything. But I was feeling heavy. I wasn't worried about my dog or my house. We had nice people looking after things. It was something quite different.

I prayed about it and soon discovered that it was my family I was missing. Yes, I missed my biological family very much but it went beyond that. I missed my spiritual family. I wondered what was happening during Christmas Eve service and where everyone was spending their day. Who was traveling and what kind of joy they were experiencing with their loved ones.

I wondered, as I perspired in the eighty-degree heat, if it was snowing back home and where folks were going for our traditional Christmas Eve dinner out.

And then New Years Eve came. It's different in Florida. They sit outside and shoot off fireworks to celebrate the New Year. The people drink beer and have a "great time."

I wished I was celebrating communion and hugging my friends and wishing them a blessed 1997.

My children came inside and kissed me and hugged me. Little Alex came bopping in with her coveralls and black patent leather shoes to say "Happy New Year," and I blew a kiss to Jasmine who was dreaming through her first celebration.

Yes, this was family. Biologically bound by the blood in their veins and the love in their hearts and I am blessed to have them. My spiritual family also blesses me, also bound by blood, the blood of our

Jesus. His blood brought us together as a family that will never be totally separated. A family we laugh with and cry with, a family that pulls together through everything with a common goal of looking up, not in.

Our next year together will have a lot of new exciting things happening. We will grow in body, mind and Spirit. And we will connect together. Loving one another as Christ gave us the example with His disciples.

Oh, we'll argue and spat. All siblings do, but we'll come together in love and continue to strive for the kind of lives God intended for us to have.

As a family.

Snow

Spiderman underoos, a tee shirt, two pairs of socks, jeans, a flannel shirt, a snowsuit, mittens, scarf, a stocking cap and finally a jacket zipped up to the neck with the hood up and the strings tied. That is how I prepared my children for an hour outside in the snow. I finally got them all bundled up and started to tie the hood of my baby girl's jacket and my son piped up, "Momma, I hafta go potty."

"Me too!" a little voice said.

You can't very well be exasperated with them but at the same time you say in your gentlest voice (although you don't feel it), "Why didn't you think of that before we got you dressed?"

"Didn't hafta go then," he said.

"Me neither," said the little voice.

So off we went to the potty and then we started the procedure all over again. But you know it was worth it when they finally waddled outside with giggles and child-like wonder at the mounds of freshly fallen snow. They ate it, threw it, stomped on it and tried to catch snowflakes on their little pink tongues.

As they played I stood there freezing, waiting and hoping they would get cold (fat chance) and want to go in where it was warm but they were having so much fun I knew we were out for a while.

"Oh man," my husband had said when he woke up that morning. "Now I have to go out and shovel the driveway and sidewalk. I'll bet the traffic is going to be horrible today. The drivers in this city are so panicky, one little snowflake and its break light city.

Yeah, I know," I said. "It will take forever to get to the store today and we need milk."

Isn't it interesting how, as we get older, our viewpoints change? I remember when I was a little girl snow meant holidays from school, ice skates, snow forts and my mom making "snow cream" from fresh snow and sugar and vanilla. I would go out and play for hours. Snow, beautiful snow.

Snow covers up the dirty environment with a blanket of dazzling white, an incredible vision of pureness. Isaiah says, "...though your sins are like scarlet, they shall be as white as snow..." The blood shed by Jesus makes us as white as snow. And if Satan comes plowing through bringing up all that dirt, a simple conversation with Jesus brings a new fall of heavenly powder to cover that sin and make us new again.

I realized I had been standing there awhile thinking of the wondrous gift of Jesus. Reveling in the freshness of His love and the covering He gave us for our sins. I felt energized and refreshed by that. I looked into my children's faces and smiled. They looked up at me with the innocence God wants from us.

"Isn't this fun Momma?"

"Yes, baby it is."

I turned around and fell backwards in the snow. Moving my arms and legs I made a snow angel. I got up and showed the children. They were excited to make their own, and together we examined our creations; a tall one and two little ones.

"Momma, Daddy's finished the driveway."

I looked at my husband. He smiled. God is so good.

"Let's go in and have some hot chocolate."

Happy New Year!

Tick, tick, tick, tick. Ten, nine, eight, seven, six, five, four, three, two, one, Happy New Year! "Should old acquaintance be forgot and never brought to mind?"

Every one gets teary eyed and hugs and kisses surrounding loved ones. But what are we expressing? Another year has past and maybe we didn't get accomplished what we had set out to do. We have a second chance, don't we? We have a new year to try, yet again, to get it right. We vow new years resolutions and plan to make our lives complete. We will loose weight, get organized, work and play harder, do those jobs we have put off and generally feel great about all the good we will be doing this new year. But by the end of February, we are back to our old habits and hating ourselves for it.

How do we get out of this slump? Do we rely on ourselves or do we rely on God? How can we expect to have a happy life without Him? Just what can we even expect to do if we don't have Someone to help us through all the trials and tribulations of this life? So many things pop up and try to destroy us as a people. Sin enters in and picks us apart with glee as we squirm and struggle hoping and praying that it would be finished. ANYTHING TO STOP

THE PAIN. But, how did Jesus feel as he hung on the cross?

Obviously He didn't beg to be let down or to ease the pain. He bore it with clenched teeth and open arms. His determination saved the world. He wasn't weak. He trusted His Father for His very life and the lives of ALL mankind. Not just those who were humble or pious.

The point is this. Jesus, being God, knew He would be scorned, beaten and murdered. He faced that horrific pain and degradation but He also faced something even more sickening. He did it knowing that many would still not accept His tremendous gift. He would offer them eternal life and life more abundantly. Being the Pillar they could cast their woes on and the Solace from all troubles. But they wouldn't accept it. "No way," they would say, "I can and will do it myself." He hung His head on the cross as He said; "It is finished." But I wonder was he thinking of those who would not accept Him? How He must have hurt. Not only in the physical but in the emotional as well. His children, those He loved and died for would walk away.

What would have happened if Jesus would have broken His resolution? What if He would have said, "What's the use?" For two thousand years now He has watched us "do it ourselves," possibly shaking His head and wiping tears from His eyes. Perhaps He asks His Father, "Why don't they get it?"

Jesus kept His resolution to die for you and me. He is the answer to ALL of life's problems. Jesus is the soothing relief that will stop the pain.

"We'll take a cup of kindness yet, for Auld Lang Syne."

Y2K

Whew! We made it through the new millennium change over. The Y2K thing. The whole enchilada. A new year, a new century and a new millennium! Did you stock up on stuff? Get ready for the bug? Think about the impending shut down of the technological world we live in? Well, I didn't either, really. We bought a couple of kerosene heaters and some bottled water and, well stuff like that. Our kids laughed at me. They couldn't believe I would buy food and water to be ready in the unlikely event that there would be need for it.

I heard stories when I was a kid. Chicken Little ran around saying; "The sky is falling, the sky is falling!" And how about the boy who cried wolf? But then again, there were the stories about being prepared such as the *Ant and the Grasshopper*. I was a Girl Scout too, and you know how those scouts are.

Everyone had an opinion about it. All the talk shows on Christian radio had something to say, the government and the military. You name a group and they were talking about it. What was a person to do? Just ignore it? But maybe it was a wake up call to a sleeping world. A world where everyone is to look up instead of down.

Wasn't it said that we won't know the day or the hour of His return? That, in a twinkling of an eye we will be changed? That we should be ready for the Bridegroom because He would come when we least expected it? Let's take a look at some Old Testament history. I'll bet Noah's cronies laughed at him. I mean, he built a boat. A huge boat in an area that didn't have much water. He was preparing for a flood. His kids probably laughed at him too.

But Jesus told us a story about lamps and virgins and being prepared for the return of the Son of Man. He showed us what would happen if we were lazy and didn't have oil for our lamps. At midnight a cry will ring out. Will we be stumbling around in the dark looking for the light while those who were prepared leave us behind? I, for one, don't want to be stumbling around in the dark.

Are you ready? Do you have enough oil for your lamp? Are your wicks trimmed? Hey! Want to compare notes? Come on over, I'll crank up my kerosene heater, get out my bottled water, and make you a cup of Y2K coffee on my trusty camp stove.

Prayers

My hamster died. He ate something that didn't agree with him; the corner of my bedroom curtains.

It was the first time I remember praying.

"God, pleeeeeeeease let Hirkimer live. He's just the best friend I have. I won't be bad and I'll be nice to my sisters and I won't ever ask of anything again, ever, not even a red bicycle. Pleeeeeeeease let him live. He didn't mean to eat the curtains. I'll do anything, God."

A little tear streaked face looking toward the ceiling hoping, wondering, pleading, wishing and bargaining. Nine year old prayers.

Then there are the prayers of toddlers. So sweet and innocent. They are said at the prompting of mommies and grandmommies and with chubby little hands folded eyes looking around they say….

"God is great, God is good…"

Prayers are beautiful. Hearing someone pray is soothing. Prayer can relax the most tense and bring comfort to the most devastating situation.

"Now I lay me down to sleep, I pray the Lord my soul to keep. Guard me Jesus, though the night, and wake me with the morning light."

We then go through a list of names. Those people we want to bring to His attention. Little ones don't miss a lick.

"And God bless Chazzy, and Pooh and Rajah (the family dogs) and..." Every living creature and some things that are inanimate deserve prayer in their eyes. Children know how to pray. They feel it in their hearts before we ever teach them. They bring all of the things they love before God in their innocence.

But He is not Santa-God or a Genie-God or the Great-Lotto-Number-God in the sky. He is our Father; the One who loves us and wants to show us, lead us and guide us. He doesn't grant wishes. He makes promises.

"I will never leave you or forsake you."

"Your whole household will be saved."

"I will send a comforter."

"Behold, I stand at the door and knock."

But you might be thinking, "God can't pay attention to me. I am only one person and He has millions and billions talking to Him. How can He hear me? Why would He want too?"

God hears our prayers, every one of them, big or small, wonderful or foolish. His ear is leaned to every one. Just as if your little one would run up to you and pull at your pant leg for attention, you would bend down, pick him up and want to hear all that he has to say.

We are more precious to God than our children are to us. Think about it.

He is listening to the prayers of His Saints.

Even the ones for hamsters.

Scaring little children

When I was a little girl, New Year's Eve was a fascinating night. We were allowed to stay up late and watch the ball fall at Time's Square on our little black and white television. My mom would fix a little banquet of treats for our "party."

We would get pretty tired waiting for the midnight hour and sometimes need to fight to stay awake for the big event. We didn't really understand what was happening when we were that young but it was special.

One year my mom was busy in the kitchen as usual, cooking and humming. We watched through tired eyes as the crowd began to count down the minutes to the New Year. A fire was burning in the fireplace and my grandmother was sitting in the easy chair looking at a magazine. Three little girls in pajamas huddled on the floor waiting and watching. My dad wasn't with us that year as with many years because he was on some aircraft carrier in an ocean someplace. But we thought of him and waited and watched. The minutes ticked by. The drone of the television and the warm fire began lulling us into a soft slumber. Nodding one by one we grew weary of the wait until.... CLANG, CLANG, CLANG, CLANG... "HAPPY NEW YEAR!" My mother shouted at the top of her lungs and banged a cookie sheet with a metal spoon scaring us half out of our wits. As we lay there, little hands on our hearts, gasping for breath, my mother and my grandmother laughed until tears rolled down their cheeks at us. We didn't think it was very funny. The New Year had been ushered in and, after we regained our wits and enjoyed our snack, each of us gave a sleepy kiss to the still chuckling women and trundled off to bed. I will never forget that night.

But in our every day lives we are being lulled into a false sense of waiting for Jesus to return. Have we snuggled down into our pajamas listening to the drone of life? Are we warm in our security, waiting and watching but nodding off?

When we least expect it the trumpet will sound...great shouts of Hallelujah will abound and the Heavenly Host will proclaim the coming of the King... "Hallelujah! The King is coming..." Will we be scared out of our wits? Will we lay there with our hands on our hearts gasping for breath? Or will we triumphantly laugh and look to the One who will take us home?

The King is coming.

Hallelujah!

February

Valentine's Day

It's Valentine's Day again. I wanted to write about love but the only thought I had was about a slimy, dirty, smelly, wet dishrag. The kind that has been lying in the bottom of the sink for a couple of days (or weeks). The one that makes you wrinkle up your nose when you take it out of the sink with two fingers.

It was clean a few weeks ago. Soft and fresh from the cabinet and probably smelling like somebody's garden or a baby or something depending on what kind of fabric softener you use.

I also thought about other kinds of rags. The rags we use to wash our car, mop the floor, wipe of spills, and the ones we use to catch drips when we clean the aquarium. We dry our dogs with them, polish shoes with them and use them for checking the oil in our cars. They are handy but dirty.

They can never clean themselves. We have to physically take them (if we can stand it and don't just throw them away) and put them in the wash. We add detergent and bleach and let them agitate to get them clean. Even at that, not all of the stains come out.

We are like rags. We work hard. We try to do what is right and will argue with anyone who says different. Sometimes we get all puffed up in our work and forget Who it is we're working for. We don't realize that we are really like a dishrag in the bottom of the sink. We've done the job of washing the dishes but we think we're all done. We washed them didn't we? We put in our two cents worth, right?

I'll bet by now you are asking what this has to do with Valentine's Day. It's quite simple; when we are laying at the bottom of the sink Jesus picks us out. He doesn't use two fingers and He doesn't wrinkle His nose. He takes us gently in His hand and rinses us in the blood of His love. He doesn't agitate us or bleach us and He never uses harsh detergents. He hand washes us as if we were delicate articles and lays us in the Son to dry. With the breath of the Holy Spirit we are made springtime fresh. Each time we are used. Not in two or three weeks. All of the stains are gone.

Washed by the blood of the Lamb.

Because He loves us.

Love

Everyday we experience love. The love of a spouse, our children, or perhaps and ice cream sundae. It comes in all shapes and sizes and can never be diluted.

One cold blustery day, I experienced an example of unselfish love. The ladies of my family and several others were gathered together to celebrate the coming of a new baby. It was a long day with many gifts and by the time we were through, everyone was anxious to go home and relax. Some of the women had come from out of town and had a long drive ahead of them.

My daughter returned to the building and told me that she had dropped forty-six dollars out of her pocket *before* the shower began and was preparing to leave a note for anyone who might have seen it.

"I've found six dollars but the rest is gone," she said. My first thought was of the extreme need she had for that money and now it was lost.

I told my mom, my sisters and my niece and kissed them all goodbye and began cleaning up. I was very surprised when I saw them several minutes later, running around the front yard of the church, hair flying crazily around on their heads. Now, it's not strange for my family to do weird things. It took me a second to realize what they were doing. They were looking for the lost money!

"They'll never find it," I thought, but to my amazement, they did. Along the fence and in the ditch! And the neat thing about it was they came out a dollar ahead! Instead of forty dollars, they handed my forty-one. A bonus buck! I was grateful, but not as grateful as my daughter.

It was an act of love. Unselfish and pure. They wanted to get back what was lost. To help someone who was in need. Jesus said, "Give and it will be given to you. A good measure, pressed down, shaken together and running over, will be poured into your lap. For with the measure you use, it will be measured to you." [1]

He didn't mean only money. He meant love. He is serious about it. There are 679 references to love it the Bible, and it all began with God. He loved us so much that He gave His Son.

His only Son.

In an unselfish act of pure love, even though we are lost, He looks for us. Perhaps with hair flying crazily around on His head, so that we might have life and have it more abundantly!

Being Number Two

The way I look at it, and I'm almost certain you do too; love comes in all shapes and sizes. We can love pets, people and even inanimate objects. But the most incredible love is the one you might have taken for granted for awhile.

I'm not talking about the relationship between God and us. Not this time. I'm talking about the no nonsense, giving all you've got kind of love that you teenagers don't know about yet and young married couples are only hoping they will experience. The kind of relationship that you know you are the center of. To have someone praying for you daily and who you want to spend every waking minute with.

In the past, I have shared my life with you to some extent. You have heard about my children, grandchildren and pets. You've seen into my family and heard me tease my brother (he's a grandpa too you know) and yet I've kept my most cherished earthly relationship close to my heart and held it there.

There is a man in my life that has literally watched me grow up. He was with me when I learned that I didn't have to cook for an army just because my mother did. Through the years he has been by my side during the darkest hours. He has been my mentor. He watched me give birth to our children and he nursed me back to health when I had surgery. He waited patiently while I regained my emotional capabilities during some of the blackest hours when I didn't think living was the answer either.

He wakes me in the middle of the night to pray and he leads me in the direction of the righteous. He guides me, spoils me, corrects me and loves me. He has a gentle spirit that enfolds me into its depths and gives me solace. I would be lost without him.

You know what my favorite thing about him is? I am second in his life. He shows me the Bible and he lives it. He brings true meaning to the following words...

"Love is patient, love is kind. It does not envy, it does not boast, it is not proud. It is not rude, it is not self-seeking, it is not easily angered, it keeps no record of wrongs. Love does not delight in evil but rejoices with the truth. It always protects, always trusts, always hopes, always perseveres. Love never fails."[2]

I hope my children experience this kind of love. This Valentine's Day, be thankful for your mate. If you aren't yet married, pray for the mate God has planned for you. Those of you who have planned to stay single, thank God for the Bridegroom He provided for you.

Love. The greatest gift given to man by our God who loves us. All wrapped up in a big scarlet bow.

Provision

My sister collects dirt. Now, I don't mean she collects it on her person or anything like that but she collects it in her house. She has it from all over the world. Not blown in by the wind or carried in by her children's shoes, but in little jars and boxes and containers. She has collected it for years.

Now if you want to know the truth, the dirt, at least most if it is really sand. White, gray, yellow and red. She has a sample from St. Croix, Virgin Islands, smuggled out by my mother after a mission trip several years ago, and from several of our United States.

She also has a passion for the American Indian. Our family has quite a lineage of Cherokee in our ancestry. So it was quite natural for me to want to bring her a present from my trip to Phoenix.

My companion and I traveled for miles looking at the countryside. As far as you could see was desert. It wasn't the dank, hot, vulture infested desert you see on television, it was filled with cactus and tumble-weeds and beautiful earthy color. Saguaro cactus stood majestically, arms pointing heavenward like sentries guarding the base of the huge purple mountains. God's country.

We were looking for an Indian Reservation. When we arrived at the Ak-Chin reservation we pulled into a little store and spoke with the woman working there. She was plump with dark skin from the sun and had beautiful long black hair streaked with gray. Her round face smiled as she spoke to us about a tiny museum up the dirt road. I imagined her there dressed in a buckskin dress with her hair braided, instructing the settlers as they came through. I wished I had more time just to sit and talk with her, to hear her story. We drove along looking for the museum and never found it, but my goal was to get my sister her gift.

As we pulled to the side of the road, I felt the familiar lump in my throat I get when I am thinking of one of my family members and how I miss them. My heart was thinking of my Nancy, with an Indian name, PiZi Ista. I knew she would love to be there. That her thoughts would immediately travel back to a simpler time with teepees and horses and beautiful tanned people. I stooped down with my little plastic container and scooped up the sand. Sand that may have been trotted across by Sitting Bull or Geronimo, maybe a buffalo had stood there watching the horizon. I picked up a few small pebbles and a couple of sticks for my own collection and we drove off toward "civilization."

I thought about how I would present my gift to her. Maybe I could get a small beverage bottle from the plane when we flew home, but I forgot to ask. Perhaps one of my little antique medicine bottles, but no, that wasn't good enough. Then, as I was walking through a park with my little ones, I spotted a tiny Tabasco Sauce bottle lying in the grass. I picked it up and, looking heavenward, laughed with my Lord.

Chili peppers, almost a national symbol in Arizona, are what are used to make Tabasco Sauce.

God was telling me that He not only looks after the big things in life and that He is there to keep His promises, He was telling me that He looks after the little things as well. From the majestic mountains and deserts of Arizona to a tiny Tabasco Sauce bottle in Ohio.

March

110 %

In the beginning, a long, long time ago, so many years that it's hard to imagine, God created earth. The earth with such beauty and grace that it totally escapes the imagination. We all know of the beauty of the trees, oceans, wildlife, birds and flowers. This was created perfect, with much detail, because He cared enough to do His very best. But what would have happened if God hadn't cared?

At first the earth was empty and dark. God said, "Let there be light," and there was light. But when the light came on, there was such a drab and dreary place that He decided to perk it up with some flowers and fish and animals. He knew He had at least seven days to do it in so He went back to bed and decided to wait for the next day. This went on for six days and on the sixth day God said, "If this earth is going to be created in a week, I will have to do it today so I can rest tomorrow."

He chose the waters of the earth first. He commanded the waters to separate and dry land to form and the sky to be sky and it was okay but not His best and He was not happy. He went on however, because He was behind schedule and He had to hurry. Next He began working on the plants and flowers. He knew there should be many different kinds but, being in a hurry, He only made oak trees and purple daisies, nothing else. Lots of them though to take up space. He knew there should be seasons but to cut down on time, He made summer and winter. No spring or fall. He made the sun and moon but He made the moon too bright so He threw a huge sheet over it to make it darker. By now he was really looking at His watch. Time was almost up and He hadn't made the animals or food or anything. So He said, "Let there be trout." And all the waters of the earth held trout. "Not good." He thought, "but I have no time." He went on to create birds, but instead of millions of different kinds, He only made pigeons. Next He decided to make some animals. He new there should be many kinds but He made some Hippo's and some lions but nothing else.

He was getting very tired by now and said, "Why do I have to do all the work? I don't like this!" He realized it was eleven o'clock and He hadn't created anything that looked like Him. Hastily He created man. "Let's give him one eye, he only needs to see, not see everything. And one ear and he needs to be warm in winter so Let's cover him with lots of hair and in the summer it will fall off and…well…okay here's a mate for him but she only gets one of everything too.

When He had gotten this far He realized that He needed food for His creations. He gave the animals grass, the trout algae, and the bird's seeds. Then He thought about man. He said, "Here are a cow, some asparagus, and a pear tree. There is one apple tree in the oak woods but don't touch it."

Now can you imagine a world of winter and summer, only oak trees and purple flowers, a moon with a sheet over its head and people with one of everything who are hairy in winter and naked in summer? Can you also imagine eating only beef, asparagus and pears your whole life? And only trout and pigeons to look at as well as hippos and lions? This is what would have happened if God had only given a little of Himself. If he hadn't cared to do His best.

Do you do your best in what you do or do you hurry up to rest or play? Do you give up because "It's not my job," or you think it's stupid? Maybe we should give our best. Maybe we should make it our job. And maybe, even if we think it's stupid, we should do it anyway, 110%.

St. Patrick's Day

"**Y**ou tell us that there are three gods and yet one?" the puzzled Irish folks said. St. Patrick was preaching the gospel to them in the 5th century AD.

"How can that be?"

The saint bent down and plucked a shamrock, "Do you not see," he said, "how in this wildflower three leaves are united on one stalk? And will you not then believe that there are indeed three persons and yet one God?"

According to Irish legend, Ireland's patron saint chose the shamrock as a symbol of the Trinity of the Christian church. To this day the shamrock remains the national emblem of Ireland and is worn proudly by Irish people the world over on St. Patrick's Day.

Why follow Irish legend? The true story of Saint Patrick is simply this; Patrick was born to a Romanized family in Britain probably in the first half of the 5th century. He was 16 when he was taken by pirates and sold into slavery. He was sustained by faith during his six years of working as a herdsman. When he escaped and returned to Britain, he had a vision of the Irish beseeching him to return to Ireland to spread his faith. After studying in continental monasteries, Patrick returned to Ireland as a missionary. Despite constant threats to his life, he traveled widely, baptizing, confirming and preaching, building churches, schools and monasteries. Patrick succeeded in converting almost the entire population of Ireland.[3]

Wow, what an incredible man. He went out and converted almost all of Ireland for Jesus. Sometimes we have trouble even speaking to our neighbor, much less sharing Jesus with them. Struggles are hard, but with faith, perhaps the faith of St. Patrick, we can do it. So, contrary to popular belief, the Irish aren't only brawlers, drinkers and leprechauns, we can be Christians too.

CAT

I gave my cat a bath the other day.
Needless to say, she didn't like it one bit.

Now you may ask why I would do such a crazy thing as that especially due to the fact that she still has teeth and claws, and my answer to you is this; she has a skin problem that we are unable to figure out. She itches, gets infected and is downright miserable. I love her so it makes me sad to see her in this condition.

I got the shampoo and rinse I had just bought from the vet, a towel and took off my jewelry in preparation of bathing my little kitty.

"Cat," I said softly.

"Come here Cat." Yeah right. You know cats. She wouldn't come even if I had a great big juicy mouse to give her. I picked her up and headed to the sink. This would be great. I had given her a bath before and lived through it. What I hadn't counted on was her unwillingness to cooperate and the possibility that she was in a bad mood in the first place.

Perhaps the shampoo irritated her somewhat or maybe she was in just a plain nasty mood. The claws came out and the blood started to flow.

I got a better grip on her and tried again speaking soothingly to her and rubbing her face with my thumbs in an attempt to comfort this now very wet soapy, ferocious animal.

The sharp agonizing pain that shot through my finger caused me to release her and go for the anti-bacterial soap to prevent infection from the major injury just inflicted from my "little kitty's" teeth.

I called the vet.

She said that at the very least I had to rinse the cat completely. To make a long and very painful story short, the cat won.

Or did she?

As I sat nursing my wounds I wondered why she would react like that to me. I was only trying to cleanse her of her affliction. I wanted her to feel better, to live a life of freedom from her pain and agony. I wanted her to realize that I was her caregiver and the one who could save her from her torment. I even let her hiss at me. She scratched me and bit me. She hurt me and made me bleed. But I still loved her.

Then I had a most humbling thought. "Even though He was pierced for our transgressions, He was crushed for our iniquities; the punishment that brought us peace was upon Him, and by His wounds we are healed."[4]

My cat reacted just like people do when they are rebelling against God. She fought and kicked and scratched. She bit the very hand that was trying to heal her. She would rather suffer than know that love, and yes, forgiveness.

So we rebel and think, "I won!"

But did we?

Too Many Irons

It seems like there are just not enough hours in the day. From work to home to bed to work, our days are completely taken with stuff to do. We don't seem to have the time to relax and take the time to get to know those around us much less the family we are working so hard for.

Do you know, (this is a confession that will make my husband shake his head) my Christmas tree is still up? I'm serious. I didn't choose to have my tree up until St. Patrick's Day but it is and, well, it's the right color so maybe I'll just decorate it with shamrocks and leave it there until I have time to finally get rid of it.

Now don't get me wrong. My time is not SO congested that I can't take a few hours to do this menial task. I simply have more pressing things on my agenda right now. Like listening for the voice of God. Do you realize how difficult it is to hear Him speak to you when there is so much confusion and noise around? It's hard. God is trying to speak to us but we are running around in circles trying to catch our tails and He can't get us to focus for even a minute. And then we cry out, "God, why aren't you listening to me?"

He is. He want's to answer our every question if only we will stop for a minute and lend an ear. Turn off the radio. Walk in the woods. KILL YOUR TELEVISION, and listen. He has a still small voice that roars like a lion. He is moving and He wants us to follow.

In a world of instants, instant food, one-hour photo, drive through pharmacies and five-minute puddings, just remember; God is a crock-pot. He takes His time to get things done right.

Protection

My guardian angels have bruises on their shins. I just know they do because I was the cause of them. I felt them bump the last time I got my car too close to the one in front of me and if I put my spiritual headphones on, I probably would hear them say, "Ouch! I wish she would calm that type "A" personality down and drive like a normal human!" I am sure they are kept busy protecting me from the dangers of life.

Protection. A word we hear at least a hundred times a day either on television or the radio. We might even be hearing it in the classroom and at work. We seek protection from disease, emotional pain, financial ruin, and just plain life. Everyone seems to be thinking protection to guard their lives.

Why even the toothpaste my little granddaughters use proclaims, "call poison control if accidentally swallowed." Come on now, how many of us have swallowed toothpaste in our lives? Be honest, it's not something we look forward to doing but, hey, it happens. And when you are teaching a small child to brush its teeth, the goal of the child is to suck all of the toothpaste off of the brush! It's almost like the gag (no pun intended) I heard stating that saliva causes cancer, but only if swallowed in small amounts over a period of years. I am sure the toothpaste companies are just trying to make sure we (here is where I clear my throat) are safe.

My point? We constantly scurry around safeguarding our children running to and fro in an almost futile attempt to keep them from being hurt in any way shape or form. We are trying to be their guardian angels.

Oh sure we are supposed to teach them and "protect" them but what happens to us? If you are like me, and I believe most mothers are like this, we want to protect our children from everything. But as a result, what are we really teaching them?

When they are small we scoop them up and hold them and pray for them. But when they begin to get older, do we teach them how to call on the Heavenly Protector?

God wants to be our Safeguard. He has thousands of angels He keeps around for just this reason. They bump their shins and probably grow weary trying to keep up with us in our attempt at life. In the past year alone, I have felt angelic hands cover my mouth when an unknown disease is coughed into my face. They covered my hand when an evil presence wanted to shake hands with me. And when people of questionable intent show up in my office and I am alone, I'm protected. And if powerful machinery goes haywire and I am the only one who can turn it off, I know I'm guarded.

We are supposed to go through the "scrapped knees" of life. It helps us to grow and to learn how to fight the good fight. It is only when we remember our "protection", the power of prayer that will bring our angels. It helps them stop cars on a dime and let's us swallow the toothpaste we call life.

Erin Go Bragh!

Ah, shoren enough, 'tis the time of the year that my strappin' husband is runnin' fer cover.

He's of the opinion that Irish folks are daft. All we do is drink and cuss and fight. (Well, maybe in another life!)

But *I* am of the belief that the *Irish* are God's chosen people. I mean after all, He chose beautiful Irish lass to be the star of His angel show didn't He?

The cool color of green and the rolling hills of Ireland are my idea of Heaven with melodious music and soft breezes flowing over the sea. What an incredible sight to behold.

I can imagine a majestic white horse galloping across the meadow, running for the shear fun of running. It's mane flying in the wind. Forgetting about the troubled world it has left behind. Experiencing freedom like no other.

As he comes to the shore, he looks out over the crystal sea with anticipation. A great cleansing breath fills his lungs as he waits for the shining Star. Together they begin a journey that will take them into forever.

The horizon shows a brightness that can only mean the coming of the One for whom he waits. He throws his head back and greets his Savior with an equine shout of praise. Rearing up on his strong legs he paws the air in a salute to his Rider. They will become one. The Rider will vanquish the evil one.

"I saw heaven standing open and there before me was a white horse, whose rider is called Faithful and True. With justice He judges and makes war. His eyes are like blazing fire, and on His head are many crowns. He has a name written on Him that no one knows but Himself."[5]

Be thou my vision. The true humble heart of God's servant. All glory is to God. To our Lord Jesus who gave us life! That we may run with abandon to catch a glimpse of the One whom will take us on to the rolling hills of heaven.

"And I saw a new heaven and a new earth, for the first heaven and the first earth had passed away, and there was no longer any sea."[6]

No separation from God. No longer any distance but the undefiled presence of the One Most Holy.

We are *all* God's chosen. We have only to accept the gift. The pure gift of life. Then we too can run across the meadows of heaven.

April

Body Taken From Grave?

Jerusalem—Reportedly the body of the Nazarene, Jesus, is missing from the tomb he was lain in on Friday.

Mary Magdalene, follower of the dead man, went to the tomb with Joanna, Mary (the mother of James) and some of the others closest to Jesus to anoint him with spices. When they got to the burial ground, the huge stone was rolled away from the entrance to the tomb donated by Joseph of Arimathea.

When the members of Jesus' group entered the tomb, the body was missing.

"Two men were there, they were dressed in gleaming clothes," Magdalene said, "they asked us why we were looking for the living among the dead. It was then we remembered the words of our Lord saying He would be delivered into the hands of sinful men, be crucified and on the third day be raised again."

It was clear the men and women believed the story. They indicated speaking with a man on the road to Emmaus who knew a great deal about the scriptures and, in deed, was the Christ. They stated they saw Him taken up and the believers are now staying continually at the temple. Public officials are skeptical about the reports from the Nazarene's people.

"Someone stole the body to make it look like a resurrection," said a soldier who requested to remain anonymous, "we did a real good job on that guy. There is no way he could have survived what we did to him."

"Yeah," another said, "we got him real good."

But this case remains under investigation. Did the Nazarene, in fact, rise from the dead as he told His disciples he would or is it some weird ruse to make it look that way?

This reporter believes Jesus. There is no other explanation. Seeing the faces of His believers and hearing the reports have convinced me to search even deeper for the incredible continuing saga of Jesus of Nazareth.

Too impossible to be true?

Investigate for yourself, you too will believe!

I'll Rise Again

I think it's because we don't want to believe someone would do so drastic a thing for us. We want to think so but because we are human, we don't feel we warrant a person actually giving their life for us. We hear about hero's everyday, people who throw themselves into raging waters or run into burning houses to save the life of a person in danger.

But to have a life given for us in a planned, painful, in fact fatal way causes us to either shun the gift or to become numb to the torture of it all. We tend to turn our backs on the facts, finding it just too terrifying to comprehend. The Easter Story brings tears to the eyes of those who love Him. Watching the portrayal of the crucifixion is almost more then we can stand. But what if we had been there? Would we be the one to deny Him? Would we be the one to betray Him? Would we be a Pharisee or a Sadducee? Or would we be the woman who touched His robes?

Jesus gave Himself as a living sacrifice to save us from sin and the penalty of death and Hell. He loves us so much that He endured the ghastly death of the cross. Shedding His blood to cover our sins. He died in excruciating pain with the names of each one of us on His lips. God yet man.

And on the third day, He arose! He took our debts and canceled them. Hallelujah! His death brought us life. New and clean, refreshing and crystal clear. He became the avenue for us to reach the Father. He now sits at the right hand of God and intercedes for our every breath and prayer. From the smallest to the largest concern.

He said He would rise again and He did.

The tomb was empty.

The ultimate Hero.

Reach out to Him. Touch His robes. It's His gift to you.

The gift of Life.

Hush

Never wake a sleeping baby. I have heard that saying from the time I was a little girl playing with my baby sisters.

My mom was right. When you wake a little one, the peace that was experienced in the house is now shattered with giggles and running and questions, or crying, whining and fussiness. There are occasions however, when waking our little ones is necessary. I like to do it when we have to. It's fun to rub little Jasmine's back and gently call her name.

At first she just snores on. It takes a few minutes for my voice to reach the far depths of her conscious- ness and penetrate that deep place of dreams that has her attention for the moment.

"Jasmine," I croon, "It's time to wake up."

She begins to twitch a little. "Come on Honey, you've been sleeping a long time," I say as I stroke her fuzzy head. Her hands begin to move, opening and closing and then her legs, but the eyes stay closed. "We need to go bye-bye, Sweetie."

Now a long growing stretch begins with the back arched and the arms way up over her head. The stretch looks like it feels good. And then my favorite part, her eyes open, still heavy with sleep and she quickly searches for my face. "Here I am, Baby," I say gently and then it happens she recognizes me and her face lights up in a huge smile. Then she says it, ever so softly, almost reverently, "Pappap."

I laugh and pick her up. I'm not one bit upset that she had just asked for her grandpa. I get the hugs and kisses and we begin a great time of gentle dressing and play time.

God is like that. He is gently waking our little corner of the world with soft breezes and pretty sunshine. The songs of His birds serenade us in the early morning, gently saying "its time to wake up!"

Green shoots are poking up from the thawing ground and cheerful Daffodils are bowing their heads, catching a softly falling spring rains in their buttercups.

It's spring again. Fragrant scents of new birth and re-growth make us feel energized and we take a long growing stretch after our winter's nap.

God scoops us up and we whisper, "Abba, Father" and with a laugh, He hugs and kisses us and says, "Let's go play."

Lessons Learned

One minute you're standing there enjoying life. The warm breezes, singing birds and green grass. Cars are whizzing by and you are enthralled by the sound and color of them. Each one is different. There is a squirrel scampering across the lawn and bugs of all kinds are crawling, flying and buzzing around.

As you stand there watching and learning and listening and smelling, you think life is pretty cool and then you spot it. Wet and glorious. Yes, it is full of leaves but the temptation is too great for such a little boy and with a mighty leap, you jump right into your grandma's garden pond. Up to your armpits you sink in slime and stink. It's cold and smelly and as your mom runs over to pull you out, you begin to cry. How did life turn so wrong with one little leap?

At almost two, the simplest thing can turn a world upside down. A two-year-old takes life by the ears and runs with it. Expressing the new independence they are feeling is the most important thing in their little lives. Nothing will persuade them if their mind is set. Battles ensue and they learn and learn and learn.

But how old are we? We are told time and time again by our Father to watch out for the pit. To be kind to our enemies and to love our neighbors as ourselves. We are to hold our tongue and give without complaint. But we stand on the edge and fight the temptation to jump.

Just as the mommy ran to pull the little boy out of the muck and mire, God is there to help us not to jump in the first place. Yes, we are tempted and the amazing thing is that when we become two years old again and want to assert our independence, He pulls us out and helps us to try again.

Some of us learn. Some of us don't. But He is always there to dry our tears and wash us in the beautiful blood of His love. He knew we would be two for a very long time, but He loved us anyway.

Good Job!

When children are small, they mimic everything we do in an effort to learn the skills they will need in life. They learn to walk, and talk by watching us. Good habits, bad habits and all the habits in between. That's why it is so important for us to try to stay within decent boundaries for them.

While driving down the road the other day, I got cut off as usual, and my first instinct was to shout, "You Jerk!" But, just as I got the "You" out, I realized two of my little grandchildren were sitting in the back seat listening. Thinking faster than I drive, I finished with, "child of God!" Thus keeping my reputation fairly clean with the kids and allowing them a better recourse than calling someone an unpleasant name. I only wish I could use that restraint when they aren't with me.

Then I realized, while washing my hands in a restaurant restroom one day, Jasmine was watching every move I made. She watched me wet my hands under the faucet and she did the same. Then I applied soap and she did the same. I scrubbed my hands, making lots of bubbles, and she followed suit. Then I rinsed them, starting at the wrists and working down the fingers, (all medical people are trained to do it this way) and she attempted to do the same. We dried our hands carefully; palms and then one finger at a time, and threw the paper in the trash.

As I watched her, I realized she was carefully scrutinizing my every move. She wanted to do it just like me. I was doing it right and she wanted to learn how.

It is born into children, the need to be like the ones they love. To reach for new heights and achievements in their worlds. They live for the praise of "Good job! Give me five!"

But once we're grown, who do we look up too? Movie stars, sports figures, politicians? Or do we stretch ourselves to be like the One who is a Father to us? Are we watching? Reading? Talking to Him? How are we learning to be just like Him?

When we get to heaven, will we have watched enough? Will we be eager to face Him, or will we slink back and hope He talks to the others first?

Because of Him, you will be in heaven.

Living for the words, "Good Job! Give me five!"

What's In It For Me?

It's been said that in Ireland if you catch a leprechaun you will have good luck forever. At the end of the rainbow there is a pot of gold and four leaf clovers bring you luck. How about hanging a horseshoe above your door or putting a lucky penny in your pocket? And there are a lot of crippled rabbits limping around because people actually want their feet! Crystals are hanging in cars, around necks and every other place to get luck, love and power.

In our society, we have a "What's in it for me?" mentality. We all want riches, romance, youth and power. Those are the things that seem to matter. And what about the saying, "The one with the most toys at the end of the game wins." does that make sense?

If we would take a long hard look at what we have in our "charmed" lives, we might understand why a "what's in it for me" attitude is not such a good thing. We all have nice houses and clothes and food and video games. There are good schools and families who love us. We have people we care for and clean houses without roaches and we can take a shower whenever we want. We can wear a new outfit every twenty minutes and call our friends on the phone and eat pizza and drink pop and do just about anything we want. Some can't. Some people depend on the charity of others to provide food and clothing and to supply a place to lay their heads at night.

These folks have to worry about catching bugs from each other and where they can wash their clothes and if they are going to have a bed at night. They are in failing spiritual health and questionable physical health. But the one thing I have noticed is that a lot of them are able to trust God in all they do. Oh sure, there are those who don't know Jesus and there are those who are being lead astray by false religions, but these people rely on Christians to bring them what they need to exist.

How many of us spend countless dollars trying to win the lotto? How many of us are too lazy to walk to the kitchen for a drink of water? How many of us gripe if our hair doesn't look just right or we get a zit?

Jesus said, "If you want to be perfect, go, sell your possessions and give to the poor, and you will have treasure in Heaven. Then, come and follow me."[7] Jesus doesn't want us to have "things." He wants us to have LIFE. He doesn't want us to rely on charms for good luck; He wants us to rely on Him for all we need. And what good are riches on earth if we don't have treasures in Heaven?

Think about it. If you don't have Jesus in your life, you are doing all of this for NOTHING.

May

Mother's Day

It is that special time of year when all of the flowers and trees come to life in an explosion of color and grace. The time when new creatures are coming into the world in great abundance with chirping, squeaking, chattering, squealing, quacking, neighing and crying. Mothers of all species are responsible for the symphony of noise that is around us throughout the year.

There is nothing like the love of a mother. Mothers are soft and sweet (most of the time) and they smell good. At least mine does. They worry if you are too cold or too warm, they bring you chicken soup when you are sick and give you heck when they don't know where you are. They loose sleep over you, cry over you and pray over you. Mothers can scold you for something you have done until you are a grandmother yourself but it is only because they love you.

My mother is my best friend. She helps me through the rough spots in life with a smile and a hug. She is always ready to go when I want to "play" and she rarely thinks of herself. This is the kind of mother I hope I have become. Someone who understands and is forgiving. Guiding but not conquering.

Celebrating Mother's Day is a tradition that falls in May. Isn't that nice? But shouldn't every day be mother's day?

My mom gave me her life because she chose to give me mine. And for all of those reasons I gave her cause to pull her hair out and she didn't, I thank her. And for the times she prayed when I didn't know, I honor her. Whether your mother is near or far, let her know just how much she means to you.

"Mommy Things"

Do you know how hard it is to realize you are a mother, no…a grandmother, when you only feel twelve inside? Where did it all go? All the living we are supposed to do in our childhood? Playing hopscotch and jump rope with our girlfriends and running from the boys. When did we stop running? When did we let them catch us and marry us? When did the babies start coming? It all seems like a blur to me but on the other hand, check this out.

I have been blessed with two beautiful baby granddaughters. Granted they are not much on playing hopscotch yet, their little legs don't hop too well, but with a grandmother the age of twelve, hey, they have it made! Now don't laugh. Especially you Ric, but I can hold my own. I guess I am just spending time this year looking forward and looking back. Forward brings me to the future and teaching my daughter the same "mommy things" my mother taught me, and her mother taught her. Further down the road, Jasmine and Alex will teach their children should the Lord tarry. Looking back, I see my mother and her mother teaching my sisters and me our "mommy things".

Generations after generation mothers have gone out of their way to make life easier for their daughters. Teaching everything from cooking to mending and, do those home remedies really work. Castor oil and onions under the bed. Tie a sock around your neck and Vick's vapo-rub up your nose. Does a bellyband really take care of an outie? Let's find out.

Today marks the end of an era. My little girl will be more grown up than even five weeks ago when she gave birth to my granddaughter. She will become a wife. My motherly advice will now be passed on to the next generation as my daughter steps into her next phase of life. She will have a new baby, a new husband and a home to care for. I want to do it for her, because that is what mothers do, but I realize that she is a woman of her own and now I have to give her totally to the care of God and that darn boy. Together I know they will care for her and keep her safe as only I thought I could do. But it's time. I only pray my experiences in life have given her a good foundation to begin her journey. To be a Proverbs 31 woman and to train up her child in the way she should go.

Today I am not loosing a daughter; I am gaining another son. I will hold my head up high just as all my mothers before me and realize that this is the season for growth and continuation of Gods perfect plan. To say, "I love you, Lizzy, and I pray for your happiness. Work hard, love hard and be forgiving. Mommy things. Hug a lot and over look the little things. Hang on to finger prints and jelly kisses because, before you know it, you will be a twelve-year-old grandma."

Joy's of Motherhood

There are few joys in life as fulfilling as wiping cake batter off the walls.

"Mommy, I'm bakin' a cake!"

"Why yes you are honey, now DON'T PULL THE BEATER OUT OF THE CAKE MIX UNTIL YOU TURN IT OFF!"

See what I mean?

Cake batter is dripping down the walls and cabinets and you have a beautiful hazel-eyed cherub waiting to have her face, hair and hands washed.

"Okay son, I'm going to hold on to the seat…"

"DON'T LET GO…"

"I'm not going to let go until you're ready."

"I'M NOT READY!!"

"I know, (pant pant) you're not ready…"

"Um, OKAY MOMMA, I THINK…"

"You're ready!" as I gently let go of the seat his little sister jumps up and down clapping her fat little hands in delight as he weaves and wobbles down the sidewalk.

"LOOK MOMMA, I'M DOIN' IT!" he screams.

"Yes baby, I see you," I yell as I try to catch my breath. My little daughter runs up with out stretched arms and I catch her up and toss her into the air. She giggles and I turn in time to see my son fall off his bike into the grass. I'm a little alarmed but he gets up and brushes himself off and laughs wildly at the fact of riding his bike all by himself.

"Me next momma."

"No honey, you are still too little. We have to wait until you grow just a little bit more."

"OK momma," she says and wiggles to get down. She runs down the sidewalk trips and falls and I run to her. I wipe her tears and survey the damage to her knee "We will go get a Band-Aid Sweetie, you will be okay."

She sniffs and wipes her eyes. I call to my son to be careful as he climbs back on his bike yet again to master his new challenge.

Band-Aids and bicycles. Jump ropes and G. I. Joe men. Dolly's and dirty faces. Dripping cake batter and frogs in the pockets.

Motherhood.

There is nothing like it. The joy, the tears. I have heard it said that when they are little they step on your toes and when they are grown, they step on your heart. It's true.

We all suffer growing pains. We learn to accept the challenge of life without training wheels and to dry the tears of pain as we stumble and fall on life's hard sidewalks. We get up, brush ourselves off and try again.

Isn't it wonderful to know we have Someone who will hold on to the seat while we get our balance? Someone who will never get tired of running with us? And when we fall, Someone to put a Spiritual bandage on our hurts?

"There honey, isn't that better?"

"Yes, momma."

"HEY MOM," my son yells as he slams the front door. (I don't think little boys know how to speak softly.)

"CAN I GO SHOW MY FRIENDS HOW I CAN RIDE MY BIKE?" do you believe he is standing two feet in front of me?

"You may go for half an hour, I'll call you for supper."

"OKAY, THANKS MOM!"

In a sudden and rare exhibit of affection he runs back and gives me a grimy kiss on the cheek. I'll take it.

"Momma?" Little hazel eyes says.

I look down into that face.

"Can we go bake a cake?"

Music

Three little girls in pink sundresses all dressed exactly alike. Pink sponge curlers had adorned their hair the night before and now each one sported bobbly curls that shown in the sunlight. They posed for pictures. They were so cute. A stark contrast to the muddy blue-jeaned, bare-footed urchins they had been the day before. Tomboys every one. But their mother knew under all of that dirt there were three pretty little girls and she was so proud of them. That mother worked hard to keep her little daughters healthy, clean and educated. For every fistful of mud they encountered, she had sewn a new little dress for them. She cooked and cleaned and loved and disciplined. Hugs were incessant, spankings frequent enough to form those children into good citizens. Their home smelled of fresh baked pies and Pinesol. And there was music. Always music. When the radio wasn't on, the piano was being played and the little girls were introduced to all types of music. Their house was always immaculate; the floors shined and never was there a cobweb or dust bunny. The little girls played in the fields surrounding their home and always came running when their mother called, "Time for supper!" The mother was tired. She was doing it alone.

Life changes and so did the little girls. They went through typical teen-aged rebellion and stages of defiance but the mother trudged on hoping and praying that her little girls would soon settle down. They did. Now the mother had a new goal. Grandbabies! She cooked and cleaned and loved and disciplined. Hugs were incessant and spankings unnecessary. Her home smelled of fresh baked pies and Pinesol and there was music, always music. She sang and hummed and played with her grandchildren.

Life changes and the grandbabies grew. The mother had a new goal. Great grand babies! She cooks and cleans and loves and has forgotten discipline. Hugs are glorious and spankings unheard of. Her restaurant smells of French fries and hamburgers and there is music. Always music. She has worked hard. A lifetime of cooking and cleaning and loving and nurturing. And she is blessed. But not as much as we are.

Calluses

They can appear on your hands, feet, elbows and knees. Just about everywhere there is pressure for extended periods of time. Being in the medical field, I've seen some Mount Everest sized calluses. Huge. They run deep and can be a nuisance. Did you ever look at a farmer's hands? They are pure calluses. Hard work in rough weather causes it. Calluses are one of God's inventions for protecting the body.

I watch my little grandchildren play outside in their bare feet and remember the bottoms of my feet when I was little. Shoe leather wasn't as tough. We never wore shoes and socks. After all, who wanted to take the time to remove them when an inviting creek came into view? Those kids will have calluses on the bottoms of their feet by the second week of summer.

Then I think about the fingers of a guitar player. Those fingers are tough. Pressing the strings of the guitar time after time causes the natural protection to develop. It feels better when they do.

But the calluses I have in mind are the ones on my mother's knees. Yes, she could have developed them scrubbing floors or chasing marbles with the kids but her calluses came from a life time of praying. Praying that I wouldn't bring home a punk rocker boyfriend or drive too fast or skip school. She prayed that I would be safe when she wasn't around and that I wouldn't kill my sisters. As I grew from infant to teenager her calluses thickened with repeated use of her knees. She never told me this, but I know. I know because I have them on my knees too. It starts from the moment the precious gift of a child is known. From "Thank you God for my little baby" to "God please let them pass math." Mothers have passed prayer calluses from generation to generation.

Now naturally, no woman wants people looking at her knees to see if Mount Everest is there. It doesn't sound very attractive. But I can tell you God sees them. He knows that, each time a mother hits her knees, she means business. After all, these are her children. With due respect to God, she is entering into His throne room to say, "Excuse me but did you see what my kid just did? Oh Lord, what am I going to do with that boy? If he (or she) doesn't settle down I'll be white headed." Or how about, "Father, she's so sick. Please heal her." And "They broke up and now she is so sad."

God is sitting there nodding in understanding. He knows a mother's heart because He created it. He knew that there would be tremendous amounts of motherly noise coming from earth to reach His loving kindness. He lends an ear to listen to her, but it's the answers she's given that cause us to grow up properly. Because she takes the time to develop calluses on her knees, we don't develop calluses on our hearts.

New Birth

I t's fun to watch young mothers look at their children with perplexed gazes. They try to figure the little ones out and just when they think they have it, POW!, off the tot goes in another direction.

I have had the privilege of watching my two daughters give birth in the past few months. It was quite an amazing site to see the two girls I have watched grow up, give birth to two girls they will watch grow up. It's an unending circle. "Circle of Life." (They ought to make a movie about that.)

The two experiences were the same but different. The first birth, to my daughter-in-law, was interesting in that I could watch her react to *her* mother and watch *her* mother try to comfort her. Nervous laughter sounded in the room, dim lights, and the sounds of a new life being pushed into the world. When it was over, there was such a sound of joy. Baby crying, new mom crying, new grandma's giggling. It was a wonderful experience.

Then there was my daughter. She was willing to take a stab at the natural child birth thing. I think she wanted to try it because she knew her foremothers did. It couldn't be that hard, could it?

But the shoe was on the other foot for me. Although she had given birth before, twice, I was concerned about her. I admired her for her strength. I knew from first hand experience what she was suffering. I didn't want her to hurt but I wanted to support her decision to try. It was long. It was hard. And drugs had to win out in the end for both their sakes.

But isn't that the way it is all through this journey? We watch our children grow and taste life, and we watch them struggle with the ups and downs of childhood as they try. Mom's hope and pray and teach and heal and love. Unconditionally. We hurt for them, we weep for them, and we pray that their trials won't be too hard. It's a cycle that has gone on for thousands of years. It's a struggle, but there is One who is doing all of those things right along with us.

He watches us.

He knows it's hard.

He knows it's long.

But He respects our desire to try.

Skinned knees, bloody noses, stubbed toes and crushed hearts, crying babies, dirty dishes and hungry husbands.

The joy of being a woman is an intricate part of the circle of life.

June

A Tribute to dad

In May there is a tribute to mothers. It is only fitting that in June, we have a tribute to fathers. I mean after all we couldn't be mothers if there weren't fathers, right?

Sometimes fathers are brisk, only giving what is needed, mostly money, to the off spring they sired. But most of the time fathers act bristly on the outside but are big softies on the inside. They only want what is best for their children but secretly hope the wishes of the child take place as well. Fathers for the most part, are proud of their children. They pray that they will do their best. They know that the child has what it takes hidden somewhere in that scruffy head as they watch them scamper off to school every day. He hopes his children will carry on in his name and do something bigger and better than he did. Dads constantly push for the best.

Sons of fathers seem to receive the lion's share of the pushing. They will be fathers too someday, and the bread winners. So they are taught and groomed to do things that may seem impossible.

Daughters on the other hand, at least in some instances, are watched like hawks in the event that some darn boy will come and carry them off without so much as a backward glance. Little girls can wrap their fathers around their little fingers with not much more than a smile or better yet a tear. Dads hate tears.

A father will worry about the important things in a child's life. How they will turn out. What will they be when they grow up? Will they be able to take care of themselves? Who is she dating this week and will the car come back in one piece? They set curfews and limits all as a part of guidance for the next generation of people that will someday be in control.

As for now, well, let's go to the boy's ball game, and, it's okay for her to get her ears pierced twice but no more than that.

Fathers. We fear them, we respect them and we love them. Biologically any male could be a father. It takes strength, knowledge, perseverance, lost sleep, money and LOVE to be a Daddy.

So the next time you hear someone yell, "You're going out with Mohammed WHO?" or "You did WHAT to the car?" Remember that this is someone's hard working dad.

Father's Day

Ah, Father's Day. What to give him. A tie? How about an electric razor? Maybe even a... Well let's face it. All of us are at a loss as to what to give our fathers on Father's Day.

We all have a father. Biologically we had to have one. None of us would be here without them.

I have been blessed with four. My Heavenly Father, my natural father, my stepfather and my father-in-law. Three are unique in their own right, having in common age, wisdom and an enduring lifetime.

Of course my Heavenly Father can't possibly be included in this group. He is the most important Father in my life. The One I run to in times of trouble and the One who showers me with blessings. He teaches me and guides me and loves me unconditionally. He is the One.

My natural father. The one whose genes I have running through my body, the blue print God has given me has also taught me many things. He taught me to work, HARD, and not to grumble. He made me persevere and strive to achieve my personal best. He may have had coarse ideas and means to reach his teachings but they were there and I am thankful for them.

My step-dad is fun. I am comfortable being myself with him. He laughs with me and cries with me. He takes the time to sit on the porch and play checkers with me. He sings and dances and laughs and loves. He makes my mom laugh too. He has taken us into his heart as his own and allowed us to feel the love and nurturing that soothes our hearts.

And how about fathers-in-law? Every one of them has had to surrender his child to someone else's family and allow them to grow and mature into adults of their own. My father-in-law is a very quiet man with a peaceful strength about him that I admire. He is of German descent and has the gumption to show it. When he speaks he does so with eloquence and knowledge. He loves in a distant sort of way and he has never come against us for decisions we have made. He raised a wonderful son in whom he instilled his strength and loyalty.

Each of these men has my admiration. They have shown me love in many ways and I have become a better person for the many lessons they have taken the time and patience to teach me.

Togetherness

My dad had a vintage three-wheeled motor-cycle, a Harley I think, and it was a project we worked on for many hours.

It sat in front of Roush Hardware for the longest time and whenever we would go to the store, which was a big deal then because we lived in New Albany on Harlem Road, he would look at that bike and sigh and be all sad-eyed about it. My mom picked up on these signals and told him we couldn't afford such an extravagance and to just forget about it.

That was the year my dad learned just who Santa Claus truly was. The man brought the bike early on Christmas Eve and you would have thought he had hung the moon. You know the kid in the candy store syndrome.

It was very worn. Probably came from some old policeman or something. It was in need of paint and tires and a new seat.

He decided to paint it green. Not the sick kind of green but a pretty forest green. I wasn't surprised because my dad painted everything green. He sanded the old paint and repaired the rust holes; he even got laid up for a week using a sledgehammer to pound out a dent or two. He learned quickly that laying on your back under a motorcycle while trying to swing a sledgehammer wasn't a great idea.

But anyway, this bike had a trunk on the back. I guess that's were the policeman kept all of his tickets and guns and stuff. There were some handle things on top of it that we held on to when we went for rides. We loved it. He would take us up and down Harlem road just flying (or so we thought) while my mom quietly had a heart attack to see her little children at the hands of the "mad biker."

We didn't have the bike long. Dad got transferred out of state and we had to sell everything for the move. It was so sad the day they came for the bike. Unforgettable.

How many times do we get to have experiences like that? To help our dad in a project that means so much to him? Let's look at it with spiritual glasses.

Our Heavenly Father. Our Utmost Dad. When was the last time He asked you to do a project with Him? A project only the two of you could do? Didn't He create each one of us for a special purpose? A duty He specifically picked out? Maybe He wants us to paint the gas tank green. Maybe He wants us to detail the motor or paint the lettering on the tires. And perhaps He want's us to just hang on while He gives us the ride of our lives.

The next time your Dad wants to do a project with you, go for it. The closeness you will experience is beyond words. A remarkable time of one-on-one with the One who knows everything. He will teach you, guide you, and love you. Each step you take toward the finished project will be a step closer to Heavenly places.

You can bet that you will have a beautiful completion of God's work that He crafted for you. He'll show you the ropes. He knows how. And you can also bet He won't throw His back out doing the hard stuff.

Join your Dad on a project only the two of you can share.

Unforgettable.

Letting go

“**B**ut while he was still a long way off, his father saw him and was filled with compassion for him; he ran to him and threw his arms around him and kissed him.” [8]

Four years.
“Do you have everything?”
“Yeah.”
“You look tired already.”
“Yeah.”
“Are you hungry?”
“Nah, they gave us lunch.”
“I’m proud of you son.”
“I know.”
I swallowed a grapefruit sized lump in my throat.
“You’ll remember to go to church?”
“When I can. I won’t know about all of that stuff ‘til I get there. Oh hey. They gave each one of us one of these.”
He handed me a small leatherette New Testament. Maybe I could trust them with my son after all.
“There’s my plane.”
“Okay, everyone give him a kiss.”

I had taken charge again. I was ignoring the feelings in my chest. They came forward to bid him good-bye. Dad with a strong hug and girlfriend with a giggle, but little sister had different ideas. Her big brother was leaving her. She cried and cried and then cried some more.

"You take care of yourself, son. Write me as soon as you can. I'll see you soon."

"Okay, mom," he said as he walked to his plane.

A tall skinny longhaired boy who loved chains and moccasins had just given the next four years of his life to his country. With a quick look in my direction, my baby boy was gone.

It's so hard to let our children go. We want to go with them and guard them. I wanted to tell those Navy commanders not to be so hard on my son. After all he had a gentle spirit and he would work hard for them, just don't be hard on him. Let him call his mom when he wants and make sure he dresses warm and eats well.

But now, a full-grown man with some of the worst life has to offer under his belt will return. Still tall, still thin and perhaps still loving the unusual, but matured in a way he has never been before. He is a veteran a husband and a daddy. He went off to serve his county and learn about life. He survived.

He endured hardships and will have more to endure. But as much as we would like life to go easy on them, it won't. God allows us to go through the rigors of boot camp in our Christian walks to teach us about life. He wants us to develop from skinny adolescents to full grown mature warriors of God.

To have the ability to fight the good fight, full speed ahead. To be all we can be. The few, the proud, so we can aim high at the goals of God.

Our boy is coming home soon.

We've been waiting.

Four long years.

Now?

I was dead. You know the tired you feel after you have lugged twelve bags of mulch, weeded several gardens, put a new garden in and watched three kids intermittently while doing so? It was hot and it was miserable. But it meant that summer was on the way and we were opening the pool so we could spend days splashing and laughing and cooling off in the Ohio heat.

Our little grandbabies were so excited. They watched as the winter cover was taken off and as Pappap started the pump and vacuumed the bottom. We cleaned out their baby pool and filled it with water and told them they had to wait until the water warmed up some before they could swim. Twenty minutes later....

"Bubbie, can we swim now?" Alex, the three-year-old said.

"No not yet Honey, it's still not warm enough," I said.

"Oh." She said as she turned and ran off to play with Jasmine. Twenty minutes later....

"Bubbie, can we swim now?"

"No honey, it's not warm enough."

This went on all day until... "Bubbie, can we swim now?"

"Okay," I replied, and they ran off to put on the bathing suits they had been dragging around with them all day.

We went outside and I explained that they could play in the baby pool but not in the big pool. Disappointment crossed Alex's face but she played in the baby pool while she looked longingly at the big pool. She had waited all day for that pool to fill and she wanted in so badly. She simply couldn't wait. I told her, "Maybe tomorrow the big pool will be warm enough."

At three o'clock in the morning two little girls awakened me. I went to their room and was greeted by...

"Can we swim yet?"

"NO!" I said as gently as I could under the circumstances, "it's dark and the water is still cold. Mr. Sunshine isn't even up yet." They went back to sleep and so did I.

6:58 a.m. I was sleeping soundly in my bed when I felt two little hands pushing on my arm and a tiny whisper... "Bubbie, Bubbie!" I opened one eye and looked into the excited little face. "Yes, Alex?"

"NOW can we go swimming?"

They simply could not understand my wisdom in making them wait to swim in the ice cold water of the big pool. They didn't care if it was cold or dark or that no big person would be crazy enough to get into that frigid water with them. They only had one goal, they wanted to swim.

Isn't it that way with us? We get excited about a project in life and we don't want to wait. We want to plunge in and have a blast splashing around doing our own thing and not pay too much attention to the possible dangers that wait for us. When we do take the time to ask God, He sometimes tells us we have to wait. He knows that we need to wait until the time is right. Isn't it wonderful to be able to run to Him and ask, "Can we go swimming now?"

He might say, "No Sweetie, it's not time yet."

He sees the obstacles.

He sees the darkness.

And He knows the temperature of the water.

Discipline

When I was a little girl, my dad was pretty strict in most things. He had his way of getting my attention especially when I was misbehaving. There were a number of things he would do that would show me when I was wrong and I'm sure I pushed him to the limit many times. He could ground me, spank me, take away my phone privileges or simply look disappointed and I would know I had not made the right choice. He wasn't being mean; he was just trying to help me survive life. It made me sad to make my dad mad. I always wanted to make it better and, later in life; I didn't want to do anything that would be construed as stepping over the line. I did though, most of the time. He still loves me, in spite of all the gray hair I might have caused.

When I watch my son and my son-in-law discipline my grandchildren, I have to hold my tongue because, well quite frankly, it's none of my business. They have very distinctive ways of correcting their children. My son only has to say, "Alexandria," and give her that look and she melts into tears of repentance. My son-in-law will listen to an argument for a split second and then say "No." and the little ones don't argue any more, at least to his face.

They are good daddies. Each one trying to find that niche that will allow their children to feel free around them yet have that hand of control that helps them to stay within the lines. When the children have to be disciplined, punishment is swift but after the fact, love is extended and the kids run off again, a little smarter that a few minutes before.

Our heavenly Father is like that. I was standing in front of the church one particular Sunday, and I had an experience that, well, I'm surprised none of you noticed. I had been grumbling to God about the time that it was taking to put things into place for the new clinic downtown. I felt things should move faster and I was tired of waiting and, well after all I was working hard to make it work. You know the scenario. I felt it before I heard it. My Lord was angry. He was mad at me! He spoke to my spirit and said, "That is MY clinic, not yours. I will move it when I see fit."

I wanted to fall on my face before Him and repent my grumbling. It would have looked very silly to you, me falling flat. Some of you may have realized the reason, others may have wanted to call 911 and still others would have simply shaken their heads and thought about that crazy Mueller woman.

Instead I cried. From my very soul I let God know I was sorry. I wanted Him to forgive me of my complaining and hold me and show me He was still there. I realized that day, God's Sovereignty. Just who He is. It was a transformation of my soul and spirit. God is God. The I AM. He is the author and Finisher. I had a time-out. But not too long. Just like my son's do to their children, He soothed my tears and allowed me to rest in His arms.

When I got home that day I was feeling a little sheepish. I had really made God angry and He had not held back in teaching me. I wasn't mad at Him; I was in awe of Him. He had taken me to the wood shed.

I sat thinking about what had happened and as I thought, I was looking out my back window. Suddenly, for just a split second, I saw a beautiful yellow and green humming bird. It hovered over the pool and then flew away.

A special message to me from my Father that all was well. I was forgiven. Although I had felt His anger, I walked away feeling His love and a little bit smarter than I had before.

Truth

Those big brown eyes were almost more than I could take. She was standing there, little hands hanging on the chain- link fence as she pleaded with me. She didn't cry, much to my surprise, but she did beg.

She was dirty from a day of playing outside and her hair was bedraggled. My heart was breaking inside. She wanted to come to my house. She had been watching from her back yard at all of the stuff I was doing and she wanted to come "help" me. I wanted her to come too, but I couldn't let her.

You see, when I told her to go ask her mom if she could come over, she ran into the house and came back in a few minutes telling me that her mom had said, "yes." For whatever reason, that part escapes me now, I asked her mom. To my dismay, her mom had said, "No."

She had lied to me. I'm sure it's not the first time it has happened, but this time I caught her at it. I knew it, her mom knew it, and she knew it.

My first impulse was to lift her over the fence and give her a lecture about the virtues of telling the truth and then go on with my tasks. But that wouldn't have taught her anything. She had wanted to come to my house so badly, she was willing to lie to get there.

How could I handle this? How could I teach her that lying is bad not matter what the circumstance? I turned to her and simply said, "You can't come over."

"But why?" she asked in astonishment.

"Because you lied."

"No, I didn't..." she began and I stopped her. I didn't want her to lie again on top of it. The look on her face made my heart feel like it was being squeezed in a vice. She couldn't believe I had refused to let her come. I explained why she was "grounded" from my house and that she could come over tomorrow.

She begged, she pleaded, she apologized, she pouted and she moped. And all along, she was learning.

I'll bet when our Father has to tell us, "No," it hurts Him too. If it's true that He loves us myriad's more than we love each other, then He wants us to be happy too. But because He wants us to be safe from harm, He teaches us. He guides us along no matter how we struggle.

He says "No," and then turns His face so that we will not see how much it hurts not to give in. He goes on about His work and we beg and plead and pout and mope but most of all, we learn.

July

Independence Day

"Oh, say can you see, by the dawn's early light, what so proudly we hailed at the twilight's last gleaming? Whose broad stripes and bright stars, thro' the perilous fight, o're the ramparts we watched, were so gallantly streaming. And the rockets' red glare, the bombs bursting in air, gave proof through the night that our flag was still there. Oh say, does that star spangled banner yet wave, o're the land of the free, and the home of the brave."

"On the shore, dimly seen thro' the mists of the deep, where the foe's haughty host in dread silence reposes, what is that which the breeze, o're the towering steep, as it fitfully blows, half conceals, half discloses? Now it catches the gleam of the morning's first beam; in full glory reflected, now shines on the stream. 'Tis the star spangled banner; oh, long may it wave o're the land of the free and the home of the brave!"

"Oh, thus be it ever when freemen shall stand between their loved homes and the war's desolation! Blest with vict'ry and peace, may the heav'n rescued land praise the pow'r that hath made and preserved us a nation! Then conquer we must, when our cause it is just; and this be our motto; 'In God is our trust!' and the star spangled banner in triumph shall wave o're the land of the free and the home of the brave."[9]

Frances Scott Key wrote this beautiful song in the midst of a battle being fought for our freedom. Men and women who trusted God to guide them, and their dedication to the cause of freedom and their fellow man, stood for what they believed and fought, many of them dying.

We are still in the fight. Although not in the raw manner the writer of this song was, but a fight none the less. We are fighting for the freedom of Christianity these days. The country is in a flotsam and jetsam mode with wrongs being right and rights being wrong.

Battles rage in the pro-life movement, in our schools and in our government. But whom do we trust? The same God they trusted when this country began. The Alpha and Omega. The Beginning and the End.

Sometimes we become very weary of fighting the good fight but God has provided us with His strength and each other to hold us up in times of need. We can't give up. Would our ancestors?

This Fourth of July, with the rockets red glare, we should remember those who gave us this great country. Ultimately Jesus, who with His fight against sin, gave us freedom. "If the Son therefore shall make you free, you shall be free indeed."[10]

Stretch

"**H**oney, hurry up we're late!"
My husband is so patient. More often than not, I work on the bulletins or newsletters on Saturdays (and Sunday mornings!!...editorial comment by husband) being the type who likes to work under pressure.

I like to find articles and listen for Divine intervention in the prospect of a story for the front page. Sometimes it comes quickly, sometimes He takes His time.

Isn't it that way when we need something from God? "Honey, hurry up?" But sometimes we need to wait. We need to feel a little pressure to grow into the person God wants us to be. Pressure to extend us beyond our comfort zones to make a statement, if not verbally, then physically, for our belief.

The men just came back from Promise Keepers. A yearly pilgrimage taken to learn how to be the men God intended them to be. It is amazing to hear of the number of men who want to grow and take their rightful places in Gods world.

We, as women, can stretch our comfort zone by helping our men. We can attend our women's group to become more stable in our relationships with our mates and our children.

The teens need to stretch into the youth group. Going to retreats, mission trips and learning all they can to become warriors for Christ.

The little guys aren't left out either. Vacation Bible School is an excellent way to stretch. They can learn about Jesus. Even the toddlers and infants can stretch as we read to them and sing to them.

I had the opportunity to care for my one-year-old granddaughter for three weeks. I am so blessed with a tiny one who practically lived with me. I understand the meaning of stretching oneself out of a comfort zone. Having experienced this, I now know why God, in His infinite wisdom, give us children when we're young. ENERGY!

Let God give you an extra amount of energy to take care of the tasks at hand. Super naturally. To finish the job with time to spare and not have someone standing over you gently but firmly saying, "HONEY, HURRY UP!"

CLICK!

Your fingers are flying as you are inputting on your computer screen all the thoughts and ideas you have had locked up in your head for the past few hours, weeks and sometimes even years. As you type, you hum and think and get excited because you are finally accomplishing that great dream. No where else is this dream written. It's all in your head and hasn't even been drafted long hand. The thoughts come to you so fast that you elect to get them down before the creative juices dry up for the day and you have to quit from intense fatigue. You'll save it all when you're done.

As you finish the project and feel quite content, even smug about the best seller you have just written, you begin to close down your computer and screens keep popping up asking you one question after another and you're tired and all of a sudden, **CLICK**.

"Oh, my gosh." You say to no one in particular because you are all alone except for the dog. "This can't be happening to me," the dog raises her head and looks at you quizzically.

As you frantically punch keys and read windows and search files you begin to have a sick feeling in your stomach that you have lost hours of work. Deleted. Zapped into cyberspace with the poke of a finger. You want to laugh, cry and throw up all in one breath. You hang your head and say over and over again, "I can't believe it, I can't believe it, I simply cannot believe I just did that."

It is the worst feeling a creator can have. To simply annihilate something you have worked so hard on, to zap it into oblivion. Deleted. I think God must feel this way when we turn our backs on Him. To say that Jesus isn't who He said He was. To play on the other team. **CLICK,** gone, just like that.

But, there is another side. God is sitting there at His computer and He is watching us. Listening for those words he longs to hear. Someone saying, "Jesus, forgive me. Wash away my sins. Come into my life." He reaches over and pulls up the name of the saint. The list of sins pops up and God highlights them. *All of them.* Then, with a smile, He reaches over and **CLICK**. Gone, just like that.

Liberty

Its 105 degrees in the car and you are in a hurry. There are several errands to run before you have to return and get started on yet another project. Sweat is dripping off your face and you feel the crispness of you shirt wilt in the heat. You wonder why you took a shower in the first place and you just want to get your errands done and get home to the relative comfort of your semi air condition home when a little voice says, "I want to do it." You cringe slightly inside because you want her to learn to do things by herself but right now, you're faster.

"No honey, let me do it for you, okay? We're in a hurry."

As you reach for the seat belt to take over the buckling of it, the little voice gets a little bit louder, "No, me!"

"But Sweetie, we need to hurry," you say as you watch her for the fifth time try to even get the two belts together, "let me help."

"NO, ME!"

There's no hope for a compromise and you don't want to stifle her concentration on wanting to be independent so you look into those big brown eyes and say, "Hey, let me do it for you and you can push the button and get out at the store."

She thinks about it for a minute as you wipe the mascara from its resting spot on your chin, and then she says, "Will you give me a surprise?" At this point you would give her New York so the answer pleases her and you are soon on your way.

I wonder how exasperated our Father could get when we choose to be independent. He has a special blessing for us if only we would follow His directions. We say, "No, ME!" and He takes his hands off and waits for us to struggle to make ends meet.

"Here, let me help you," He says patiently, and we reply, "not yet." We struggle; we get tired and stressed. Our lives are difficult and we carry a burden, but we're too "independent" to rely on help. He wants us to learn and to go forward in His ways but we feel we know what to do without instruction so He stands by and watches us try. He knows we won't accomplish as much by ourselves but He is patient and waits. He is never in a hurry and although He has many projects to attend to, He takes His time with each of His children, to teach them to do things right. When we can't make it and finally do give in to Him, He very often rewards us with a surprise, His blessings.

He's there, He won't melt, and He want's to teach us.

Raising a child takes the patience of Job. Raising an adult takes the patience of God.

"I'll buckle the belt this time, okay?"

"NO, MEEEEYA!"

"But we're in a hurry!"

"It's MY turn!"

"Come on honey, please?"

"NO, NO, NO! I want to do it!"

"Let me help you, okay? Hey, I'll give you a surprise!"

Processes of Freedom

She was in a wheelchair. Not exactly in control of her mental faculties, and she was old. She was in search of something important. Something she had lost and she was determined to find it.

She could move her feet and, having no foot rests on the chair to inhibit her movements; she scampered along the floor propelling herself to her goal. Down the hall she went, loudly proclaiming her aim in a language no one could understand. Past the doors of the other patient's rooms to the hall that held the doors to the outside.

Alarms went off and a nurse's aid scurried off to bring the errant guest back to the safety of the home. She didn't come willingly nor did she come quietly. In fact, as she was being backed down the hall, she loudly questioned in a language we all could understand, "Where we going?"

She was only in search of her "freedom." She didn't care about her safety or that the alarm would tip off the staff, she wanted out.

Then there was another who, being at least eighty years younger, decided she was in search of something as well. They were bright and shiny and colorful, and they were fenced in. They were garden decorations that stood on little pedestals in the middle of beautiful ivy and flowers. She knew she couldn't climb over the fence and she couldn't pull the fence down. Every time she tried, her mother simply said, "No."

Determined, she processed in her little mind, how she would get to those tempting orbs. At last, she climbed up the stairs near by and over the fence into the garden. She reached out and picked up one of the beautiful balls, only to have her mother come and pluck her out saying, "NO!"

We fight for it every day, in large scale and in small scale. Our right to speak freely and openly about or faith and our God, and the battle rages on.

Fifty-six men signed the Declaration of Independence. All of them soft spoken men of means and education. *They had security but they valued liberty more. Standing tall and unwavering, they pledged: "For the support of this declaration, with firm reliance on the protection of the Divine Providence, we mutually pledge to each other, our lives, our fortunes and our sacred honor."[11]*

Just as the two ladies were determined to achieve independence, so it was with our forefathers. They gave to you and me an independent America. It cost them everything.

God wants to give us freedom too. He wants us to experience release from bondage. He wants to let us live without restraints of fences or censorship. He wants to give you an independent life. It cost Him His Son.

The Tempest

It was a very windy day. The sky was alive with billowing dark clouds. It was cool but not so cool that the water didn't look inviting. Obviously, rain was on the way.

The wind whipped the ocean into a frenzy of white crested waves and as they reached a crescendo, they crashed with a roaring hiss onto the wet moving sand. They started off in the distance as gentle swells of salty blue-black water. As they came closer and closer they caught the light was were instantly changed to sea-green mountains of minuscule plant and animal life.

There was frightening excitement swimming in the ocean during a storm. I have never done it before but I was determined to do it now. I wanted, no, needed to feel the blast of the waves against my body. I had to feel life and the ever-present pulse of the ocean against my skin.

As I walked into the water, if felt both warm and cool as the waves washed up around my knees. The air was chilly and the wind felt good against my sunburned skin. The dark clouds gave my journey a cloak of mystery. The crashing waves resisted my progress, hurling me back toward the shore. I tumbled head over heels in the salty brine. I realized then how insignificant I was and that I had to rely on something, Someone, much greater than I, to keep me on my steady course.

I thought about God and the vastness of His power and love. And as I walk through the trials of life, being constantly tossed and turned by the problems and hassles I have to endure, I have a Live-preserver right there.

Looking into the storm, it dawned on me. Life is a raging ocean of buffeting peaks and valleys. I could choose to grasp the hand of Comfort or I could be swallowed by the waves of time.

As I turned toward the beach feeling comforted and a little sore from my "work-out," I noticed the Promise that had been made so very many years ago. Hanging in the sky that had been so violent a few moments ago, was a magnificent rainbow. I knew then that whatever the trial, no matter the problem, my Comforter was right there, waiting.

August

Take the Plunge

It's sweltering. Heat permeates the very core of your being. Sweat drips down you face and back and accumulates in your hair and on your clothes. The more you wipe it off, the more it pours. Dirt and grit combine with body oils and bacteria to make a sticky, smelly mess of even the best dressed individual.

It's August.

Now imagine you are in the condition described above and have been that way for several days. Your tongue is thick and dry, and you feel like it's never going to end. As you walk along, you notice a huge pool of cold inviting water. Crystal blue and shimmering in the slight breeze that has kicked up making the hot air around you feel hotter. You walk toward the pool. It's ice cold. You know is it because you can see shivering dripping children in the area.

Do you stick a toe in? Is it a gradual thing to immerse yourself in the cold delight? How about grabbing your nose and doing on old-fashioned cannonball right into the middle of the water? What method would you use to completely surround yourself in the refreshing cleanliness of the crystal blue water? Perhaps the Nestea plunge!

More often than not we find ourselves in a spiritual desert parched from life's fires and battles. It's hot work trying to put them out. One by one they often draw us in their intensity, away from God. We are so consumed in the problem, we overlook the solution.

Just think. Jesus provides us with the oasis from which we can escape the torment of the heat.

Cool, refreshing, clean.

What would it take to get you to jump in the middle of Jesus' pool? Our minds can be overrun with the decisions of life. It isn't until someone gently reminds us that we haven't given it to God that we realize we've been going full tilt and haven't hit our knees with our situations.

When we are facing life changing struggles or even when we've lost the car keys, Jesus is there to help us find the answer. We only need to take the plunge.

Yes the water is cold. It will probably make you gasp in surprise at the numbness of it. But imagine this, in a few seconds the realization of total calmness and respite will over take you and you will wonder why you stuck in a toe to test the waters. The next time you feel like you are in the fire and life is fanning the flames, perhaps you'll remember the feeling of peace and strength that came and you will be brave enough to take the Nestea plunge into Jesus.

Atlanta

Are you suffering from it too? I know I am. It's called Olympic Fatigue and it's caused by watching the Olympics and experiencing all of the emotions of it into the late hours of the night. We laugh and cry, cheer and moan and are amazed by the feats of strength, agility and stamina that these athletes have.

They have practiced for countless hours on their sport, some of which last a mere 19.31 seconds. They paint their fingernails gold and run in gold shoes. Some of them come from far away lands we have never heard of to compete only for the competition, realizing they don't have a chance to win but maybe, just maybe.

Although most of them appear to compete alone, they are on a team and those on a team will go to extraordinary lengths to achieve the goal for that team. Kerri Strug was an inspiration. Although she was injured, she took off in flight, perhaps sacrificing her career to make the winning vault for the women's gymnastics team. She landed in agony but stuck there until she was allowed to go and then, and only then, crawled off the mat to the arms of her coach and the rest of the team. Battered and bruised, crying in pain but also in joy, she was carried to the platform where she and her team were adorned with gold. How lovingly her coach, Belah, carried her. Cradling her in his arms and as he did, he received a timid kiss on his cheek from the little girl. He kissed her back of course, beaming with pride.

I want to be like her. I want to try so hard it hurts. I want to work hard with my team mates helping the team grow and maybe to be an inspiration to others who might want to join the winners. After all, we are a team. All working together for one goal. To do our personal best only to have it benefit the Coach. Oh sure, Kerri left Belah for a time. She wanted to experience other coaches that would perhaps make her a better gymnast bit it didn't pan out. She returned to the coach who loved her and would guide her. With his gentle but firm ways, he molded her into an Olympic star.

When the time comes for the award ceremony of my life, I want to be carried battered and broken in body by my Coach. To place a timid kiss on His cheek and perhaps receive one from Him. I want to be carried to the podium having given my all, and be placed with my teammates to receive our reward.

Cook-out

Barbecued ribs sizzling on the grill with sauce dripping into the flames; making a mouth-watering scent of delectable summer food. Soaring to the heavens is the tantalizing aroma that makes you want to dive in with both hands and not worry about napkins. Hungry yet?

They make me sick. Literally. So sick that I would rather die than breathe. You see, I have always been affected that way. Whenever I eat pork, I get almost deathly ill. You are probably wondering what this has to do with a church newsletter and whether it's any of your business if I get sick eating pork or not.

I was thinking (my first mistake) about what to make for dinner Friday night. I wanted to use my grill but was sick (Ha!) of chicken and hamburgers and hot-dogs. I wanted something different. As I was driving along I spotted a sign that said, "Spareribs $1.99 a pound." That's it!

I pulled into the lot and went inside of buy spareribs. As I stood in line a still small voice (you know Who) said to me, "You know pork makes you sick." As I stood there listening I reasoned with Him. "Yes, but I haven't eaten them in a long time, perhaps today will be different." I paid for my packages and off I went to cook the world's best dinner for my family.

As I stood at the grill watching the sauce drip into the flames and wondering if I would get them done in the middle, the Voice came back. "I know those smell good, but hasn't Tim told you not to eat pork?"

I began to feel a little bit guilty. "Um, yes but aren't we allowed to eat everything now?" It's a confusing subject when dinner is about ready and you're starved.

As we sat down to the table and blessed the food, I felt the nudge again, "Don't eat that."

I ate salad and French-fries and watched as my kids devoured the ribs. After the salad was gone, I did it. I reached over and picked up a piece of charcholy brown meat and began munching. "You are going to regret that."

Uh-oh.

Isn't that the way we are? We try to reason with God as to why we can get away with something when someone else can't. Worse yet, we try to sneak one over on Him and hope He isn't looking our direction when we do it. It's a wonder He doesn't throw up His hands and say, "Fine then, just go on about your own business. You are soooo hard headed."

He let me live in spite of myself when I was hoping He would let me die, but the joke was on me. Next time I hear Him tell me not to do something no matter how insignificant I think it is I hope I have the brains to listen. It sure beats the consequences.

Ashes

Nine months, twenty-six hours of labor and a nine pound five ounce boy was born. They laid him in my arms and from that moment I vowed to protect him from everything life had to throw at him. I wanted to keep him from skinned knees and busted lips and make him into the smartest boy the world has ever seen. The moment I kissed the top of his downy-soft strawberry-blonde head I was smitten.

As he grew up, I knew that he was a softhearted, but strong willed individual who would make his own destiny. He knew what he wanted and his ideas weren't always my ideas but they seemed to work out as I hovered around him, still wanting to keep him safe. He grew and grew and GREW! Finally, I had a young man on my hands. He met a little girl in the youth group and his Yenta of a mother decided his destiny was sealed.

But the boy had other ideas. He had a different drummer to march too. His ideas weren't my ideas and he decided on a different life. Far away. And God didn't live there. He had a home and a new family. A job protecting our country. A wife and a child. And he seemed happy. But soon that life began to crumble. His father and I began to weep and to pray and to ask God, "Why?" We couldn't understand how this could happen to our boy. After all, didn't we set a good example? Didn't we stick to our marriage through thick and thin for twenty-five years now? Didn't we seek God's face for our decisions? But through careful examination, and with much prayer, we accepted our son's divorce.

But God is a good God. He had a plan. Although our son stepped away from his Creator in the midst of his pain, the Creator never stepped away from our son. The boy who told me when he was twelve, "All I want to do when I get big is get married," began to see the little girl from the youth group. She had grown up too. She was now a beautiful woman with blue eyes and a heart for God. She invited him back to church. She invited him back to life. And although she had been hurt before, took a deep breath and invited him back to love. God smiled at this union. The "Wife of his youth." God began a new life for the young man. A life filled with love and kindness and a renewed devotion for his Savior. Beauty from ashes. A fairy tale wedding. And God said, "It is good."

Are you a Cat?

*A*nd Adam said, *"Lord, I was in the garden, you walked with me everyday. Now I do not see you anymore. I am lonesome here and it is difficult for me to remember how much you love me."*

And God said, "No problem! I will create a companion for you that will be with you forever and who will be a reflection of my love for you, so that you will know I love you, even when you cannot see me. Regardless of how selfish and childish and unlovable you may be, this new companion will accept you as you are and will love you as I do, in spite of yourself."

And God created a new animal to be a companion for Adam. And it was a good animal. And God was pleased.

And the new animal was pleased to be with Adam and he wagged his tail. And Adam said, "But, Lord, I have already named all the animals in the Kingdom and all the good names ate taken and I cannot think of a name for this new animal."

And God said, "No problem! Because I have created this new animal to be a reflection of my love for you, his name will be a reflection of my own name, and you will call him 'DOG'."

And Dog lived with Adam and was a companion to him and loved him. And Adam was comforted. And God was pleased. And Dog was content and wagged his tail.

After a while, it came to pass that Adam's guardian angel came to the Lord and said, "Lord, Adam has become filled with pride. He struts and preens like a peacock and he believes he is worthy of adoration. Dog has indeed taught him that he is loved but no one has taught him humility."

And the Lord said, "No problem! I will create for him a companion who will be with him forever and will see him as he is. The companion will remind him of his limitations, so he will know that he is not always worthy of adoration."

And God created "Cat" to be a companion to Adam. And Cat would not obey Adam.

And when Adam gazed into Cat's eyes, he was reminded that he was not the Supreme Being. And Adam learned humility.

And God was pleased. And Cat did not care one way or the other.[12]

Are you a cat or a dog? I have two grandcats and two granddogs and also have the privilege of being the "master" of a Yorkshire Terrier although I don't know to this day who the master is.

In ancient Egypt, people thought of their cats as gods. Cats have never forgotten this. If you are a cat lover, you know that cats are very independent animals. They eat when they want to, sleep when they want to, and are petted when they want to be petted and not one minute before. They purr and rub and use those soft little paws to knead the right spot to lie down in when they want to. Cats own the place. They aren't very social animals. Now don't get me wrong, I'm a cat lover too. I can't say as much for my husband who thinks the only good cat is a… well, I'll leave that you your imagination. I've heard the same thing from other men.

Dogs on the other hand, are very social critters. They want into everybody's business. They are vocal and bound around the house ready for anything the owner wants to throw for or at them. After a long day at work, a cat will vaguely recognize your entry, but a dog…well that's a whole different picture. The dog will come bounding in wagging its tail, yipping and licking and wiggling, so happy to see you. They don't care that you may have yelled at them that morning for eating you good shoes. Dogs are genuinely glad that you are home. They don't leave you when you're sick, and follow you around the house making sure you aren't going to need them for something. You're lucky to see you cat every few hours.

But, are you a dog or a cat? How do you relate to your Master? Do you rush in to meet Him, preparing for anything He has to throw at you or are you aloof and disinterested? Do you follow Him everywhere He goes or do you knead a nice soft spot to lie in until the desire to move hits you? Do you listen eagerly for the sound of His voice or yawn and stretch and settle for yet another place to sleep?

Are you anxiously waiting for a new command or do you lay there saying, "Are you talking to me… Are YOU talking to Me?"

Cats will get around to it when *they* want to. Maybe. Dogs will do it because of the rewards. The scratches behind the ears and the rubbing of the tummy. The affectionate rewards of a loving Master.

Think about it. Be a dog. Hey, who needs all that sleep anyway?

Forever

He was a gruff old guy. Kind but with an air of severity. A husband, father, war hero.

He always wanted to help others with their computers and did so unselfishly. He collected all kinds of electronic "junk" and turned it into viable pieces of office equipment. He told corny jokes, ate too much candy and was angry at God.

She is sweetness and light. Her soft-spoken nature is underlined by her gentle disposition. She is a mother, wife and a retired schoolteacher. She loves God.

An unlikely couple don't you think? They lived their lives together in the same house. Different as night and day in personality and belief. He wouldn't accept her faith and she wouldn't give up her prayers.

She loved him. She worried about his salvation. She knew he didn't have much time left and she wanted to have that assurance that she would see him again.

But he was angry at God and nothing she could do or say would change his mind. He couldn't understand why God didn't save his little daughter from the cancer that took her life. She had died several years ago and, a faithful Christian herself, stepped into the beauty and serenity of heaven. But he was devastated and he never forgave God.

His wife was calm at his wake. She said she had known it was just a matter of time. She also said that she had inoperable cancer and believed God would give her a miracle. She wasn't bitter or angry, she wasn't sad; she was just matter of fact.

She had lost a daughter, a husband and was very ill herself but she continued to praise her Lord and rest on His promises.

He never forgave God. She never blamed Him.

She knows she will be with her daughter again. They will be together forever and ever and ever.

He refused to forgive and accept. He chose to hang on to this world, his anger and perhaps thought that he could make it being a good guy.

He couldn't.

And we will miss him.

Forever and ever and ever.

September

Autumn

When you think of the word "crisp" you think of autumn. It begins gradually at first with children pretending to be reluctant to start school. Pools are closing and high school football games are being cheered on. It is a time of anticipation and readiness. The squirrels are gathering nuts for the winter, flocks of thousands of birds are high-tailing it south and farmers are pulling in crops for winter storage.

Back in the corner of your mind is a kitchen, bustling with activity. There were foods to be canned and sauces to be cooked. Smells of dill weed, sweet basil and vinegar permeate the clear, clean air. Cheerful chatter between mothers and daughters as they begin the long days of filling the larder. Apples are being made into pies, sauces and cider. Some of them are dried to be munched in front of the fire on a cold winter night. Apple butter is slathered on a fluffy hot-buttered biscuits. Pickles, jams, jellies and corn chowder fill the clear glass jars as one by one they are added to the pantry shelf.

A steady shower of rainbow leaves gently sway to the ground to become a pile soft enough to catch flying children. Father's rake to beat the band only to have mischievous little urchins run, almost silently, building up momentum until with a leap, they scatter the awaiting temptation in a hundred different directions.

It's a sweet time. Everyone is nice. It's cool enough to wear sweaters and eat chili and watch football. The grass stops growing, the pace starts slowing and creation starts to settle down for a long rest.

Beginning now the changes will be noticeable. Leaves, school buses, cooking smells, farmers, all part of the autumn slow down. Won't it be nice to enjoy the relaxing evenings? The long cool weekends? Now it's okay to sit and read a good book. And since there's nothing else to do when everything is put to bed outside, build a fire, snuggle up with someone special and enjoy the serenity.

Road Trip

I took a road trip a week ago Saturday. I was prepared with a tank of gas my praise tapes and written directions I wasn't quite sure of. I listened to the man tell me where I was going and I was relying on my memory to get me to my destination.

My reason for going to Baltimore, Ohio was that the hard drive on my office computer crashed a couple of days before. Now I'm not that had on computers. I've only had three crash in three years, but then again the reason behind this is purely spiritual and I am convinced of this but that is another story.

I headed down the highway, enjoying the sun and music and trying to relax because I was very late for this meeting. I enjoyed weaving in and out of traffic with the opinion I knew where I was going. After all, hadn't I listened to the man?

He said to take 161 to an unnamed road (he didn't know the name of the road) that was about a mile from the "State Highway Patrol" sign. I saw the sign and saw the road but I was unsure if I had gone far enough so, I did what any confused Christian would do. I prayed.

"God," I said, "I don't know the way, but you do so would you show me? I felt I should turn at the next road so I did. I drove and drove.

The more I drove the more nervous I got. I was late you know and although I knew this buy lived out in the boonies, I wasn't sure I had heard God correctly and decided to turn around. I went back to 161 and ended in Granville asking for directions.

The woman I asked wasn't sure either and I didn't write down what she did tell me. (duh!) I drove and drove. The next time I stopped, I bought a map. I followed it down and around and found Outville Road. Guess what? Yep. I had been on the right road in the first place. God had guided me there. Had I listened, I would have been late, but would have made it and gone through a lot less tribulation.

I laughed. God has a sense of humor because I'm sure He was laughing too! But, what about the more serious times in life when we truly need to hear God? Do we rely on what we have heard before without writing it down? Do we ask directions again from someone who is just as lost as we are? Or do we pick up the map and read the directions? After we ask God to guide us, do we listen or take life into our own hands again?

I think I have learned the importance of my "map" on this road trip we call life. Will we follow the directions of the Master Traveler? After all, doesn't He know where we are going?

Boycott

To Mickey or not to Mickey, that is the question. Whether 'tis nobler in the mind to boycott or to suffer outrageous lunatic behavior. Or to take arms against a sea of troubles, and by opposing end them?

In order to boycott Disney, I would have to paint my bathroom and buy a new shower curtain. We would throw out half of my grandchildren's toys, redecorate Jasmine's bedroom, buy a lot of new clothes not only for myself but for my grandbabies as well and deny that I'm simply mad about the mouse.

Now, don't get me wrong. The above paragraph could make it sound like Disney and the Mouse are idols to me and that I am placing them above God; Au contraire mon ami. I would not cry or go into a deep blue funk if my mouse stuff got lost, burned up, stolen, and obliterated by a nuclear holocaust or I simply got tired of it. I simply think that the Mouse was created by Walt Disney to provide entertainment for children, young and not so young a like. While I understand the motives behind the folks who are initiating the boycott and do agree that the "new" Disney does nothing for me, I think it is better to show the love of Christ than to constantly bring up the evil in the world. I have realized that if I were to boycott all of the places that cater to the homosexual population, I wouldn't get to eat lunch in some very good restaurants down town. Especially in German Village.

I think it's important to perhaps boycott the television shows that are bringing this type of behavior into our homes and the movies being produced by the "new" Disney corporations. Merimax being one of them. They have exhibited a strong homosexual agenda as well as anti-Christian viewpoints. This kind of stuff doesn't need to be placed right in the faces of our children or ours either for that matter.

Did you ever hear the old saying, "They are probably spinning in their grave because of that?" Well, Walt Disney probably looks like a drill bit on high speed right now.

However, to coin a new and very good phrase, "What would Jesus do?" It's kind of like the tax collectors and the thief and all of those other simmers Jesus hung around with. He didn't say to them, "Hey, I'm not hanging around with you guys because you are sinners and I don't agree with it. You better get your act together or I'm gonna really whup up on you."

Quite the contrary. He chose those types of people because He could teach them. The Bible says, "You must teach what is in accord with sound doctrine."[13]

Now I'm not saying to go to Disney World on Gay Day and try to preach to the cuddled masses but don't you think it would make more sense to start right here at home? Teaching, loving and showing Jesus? There are plenty of confused people walking the streets of Columbus. If they happen to find out you are a Christian and you are wearing a great denim shirt with a Mickey on the pocket they might say, "Hey, you must not be much of a Christian if you support Mickey." Viola, an open door!

I think that's the way God would like me to handle it. And by the way, I know some great restaurants in German Village if you want to give it a try.

Crayons

There are a lot of things to be said for crayons. They are pretty and they can make other things pretty too. Unfortunately they also have their drawbacks.

They melt in the dryer, stain walls and they don't taste good. There are waxy ones that don't color too well and then there are the Crayola Crayons we all grew up on. They were the school supply most kids looked forward to. They were the sanity of having to sit in a classroom for what seemed like endless hours learning things we would have to use in life. We were taught what our colors were and learned that there were many ways to use a crayon but no, sticking them in our noses or our mouths were not allowed. The teacher could always tell if you were eating your crayons because of the telltale purple crumbs in your teeth (not that I would ever eat a crayon).

I was very excited the year I graduated to the box of sixty-four with a crayon sharpener inside. I couldn't believe that I was the owner of such a prize. Sixty-four different colors all standing in color formation. That box even included silver, gold and copper. Priceless to an elementary school student. I never used mine. I didn't want to use them up.

I can picture God on the first day of creation. He took out His box of sixty-four and a huge piece of paper and then decided what color to make His world. Then He enjoyed the art of coloring all of life. His creations would inhabit an awesome array of beauty. He didn't have to worry about coloring inside the lines or if He would ever run out.

As He worked, He began to color man. Not just white or "fleshish," but brown and tan and black and red and yellow. Not because He wanted to compare us but because He loves variety. He loves red hair and brown hair and black hair and yellow hair and blue hair. But did you ever notice that on the inside we all have red blood? You can't see it unless you cut yourself, but it's there. It's just wrapped up in a colorful package. We're all the same on the inside. We just have beautiful color on the outside. Just like Crayola Crayons. All made of the same substance, just a different color. God had a great time creating us. He didn't use up all of His crayons and you can bet He doesn't have purple crumbs in His teeth.

Feet

What is the first thing you do when you get home? The first thing I do is kick off my shoes. It makes me feel comfortable and relaxed.

When I was a little girl, I loved to go barefoot. I would wiggle my toes in the mud, cow patties, creek water and road tar. My mom never knew what I would bring home on my feet from one day to the next. Sometimes going barefoot was painful, especially when I would find stickers, nettles or a good old thorn. But as the summer wore on, my feet became as tough as shoe leather. I could run across gravel driveways without so much as a limp. My feet would become so tough that I could even walk across snow and not feel the cold.

I have been watching the little ones in the church. They come in, shoe clad, with little socks or sandals and they run downstairs to play. Perhaps a sock and shoe-eating dragon is in our nursery because before you know it, every child comes back barefooted. They wiggle their toes on the carpet and their parents look exasperated and say, "Where are your socks and shoes?" The child just smiles, shrugs and says, "I took them off!" After church, parents go looking for the errant articles and try to put them back on their scampering offspring.

My little ones are no different. They really hate to wear shoes for very long. When we get home from grocery shopping, we make a game out of taking our shoes and socks off. Did you know that if you peel a sock very slowly from a hot sweaty little foot, the wearer will fall into peals of laughter because it tickles?

Okay you say, get to the point. Some people are uncomfortable talking about feet. God isn't. The Bible refers to feet over twenty times. It must be important to Him. In Exodus 3:5, God says to Moses, "Take off your sandals, for the place where you are standing is holy ground." And if not Moses, how about Joshua? In chapter 5, verse 15 the Bible says, "The commander of the Lord's army replied, 'Take off your sandals for the place where you are standing is holy.'" And Joshua did so. They were told that the ground they were standing on was holy.

Now in comparison, our kids don't care if the ground they inhabit is holy or not. They just want to have fun without any binding. But as they grow and learn, they will realize that, in deed, they are on holy ground. They will be grown enough to keep their shoes on, what a shame.

"...how beautiful are the feet of those who bring good news."[14] These little ones bring good news to me. They are uninhibited before the Lord. They come to Him, little shoeless children.

So the next time you see one of our barefooted cherubs, just think, "Some day I am going to be that uninhibited. I'll go to Jesus like a little child. And when I do, I'll kick off my shoes and wiggle my toes in the clouds. After all, I'll be home."

Built for a King

Once upon a time there was a little town on the coast of a far away land. The people who lived there were loving and giving, and wanted to be a part of everything that happened in their tiny community.

One day, news came that there would be a great many people who would be coming to their village. They had traveled a long time and had gone through many hardships; loss of loved ones, famine, drought and pestilence. They were weary from their exodus.

The leader of the town called the people together and indicated that there was a need for a place where the travelers could lay their weary heads and receive respite. They needed a place to call home. They needed a place to meet the King of the country.

All of the townsfolk agreed. "What can we do?" they inquired.

The leader said, "We must build a shelter. Our shelter will be fit for them to meet the King."

The people murmured amongst themselves about how blessed they were to have such a smart leader. They gave their money and their advice and their prayers.

"But who will do the work?" the group said.

"We must pitch in and do it together." He replied.

The group agreed. As they left the meeting, they began to think about the building of the shelter.

"I'm too old," thought one.

"I don't have any building skills," said another.

"I know all of the younger men will build it in a jiffy," thought yet another.

And so it went. On and on, week after week a few of the townsfolk helped to build the shelter but the majority didn't help at all. They were too busy thinking that everyone else would do it.

The leader was tired, the few were tired, the shelter was getting done but not fast enough.

Winter was coming. The travelers were coming. The King was coming. And still they plodded on.

"What is our reward?" cried the townsfolk when they were asked again for help. The leader sighed, "your reward will be in the faces of the travelers who will finally meet the King."

The townsfolk agreed.

No job was too small.

No citizen too old.

And the shelter was built with love and hard work and prayers.

Before winter.

To help the travelers.

For the King.

October

Wild Ride

Clacketty, clacketty, clacketty…. "Are we to the top yet?"

"No honey, keep your eyes closed."

"Are you sure?"

"Yes."

"What's taking so long?"

"You can't rush a good thing," he says, and I know he is smirking.

I hear snickers along with the incessant clacking noise that takes my fragile body up and up and up. Then dead silence. The clacking stops and people start to scream. I find myself falling down, down, down at a rate of speed that I know can't be good for me. My stomach is in my throat and my fingers are white from gripping the bar in front of me.

"Oh my goooooooossssssssssshhhhhhhhhhh…." I hear myself yell.

Just as I settle in my seat and thank God for the strength of my nylon seat belt, I am jerked up again clack clack clacking toward the heavens. This time I watch. This won't be as bad, will it? Practically at the speed of light we go careening around turns that throw us into the person in the seat next to us. It's a good thing I know him. Thirty-five seconds it takes to take my body from a seemingly calm state to total madness with adventure. The fear, the dread are replaced with total freedom to fly like the wind. Total trust in the guys who built that thing in the first place. Just for thirty-five seconds of fun.

But do you realize we can have that same kind of fun without even leaving the ground? I mean the knock down, turn around ride we call life. We can choose to keep our eyes closed as we enter the race but what will we miss? Perhaps getting to meet the guy sitting next to us. So when we careen around the corner and smash into him, he will understand and maybe even laugh. And how about this, TRUST. We will go and spend hundreds and perhaps thousands of dollars on adventures, trusting those who built, engineered and piloted our thrills but what about trusting the One who pilots our life?

Picture this; "Okay God, are we to the top yet?"

"No."

"But when God, when?"

"Keep your arms and legs inside the car at all times. We are not responsible for lost or stolen articles. Stay in your seat and be absolutely sure your lap belt is secure."

"Take a deep breath and trust Me."

Clacketty, clacketty, clacketty….

"OH MY GOOOOOOOSSSSSSSSSHHHHHHHH H!"

Joining Hands

Little bobbing curls, bright red-gold in the sunlight. A small head thrown back, laughing in joy. Next to her a tinier blond head running along on short blue-jeaned legs, trying hard to keep up. They are holding hands. The older one encourages the younger one to "Come On!" They are dressed in sweatshirts, blue jeans and tennis shoes and they are having the time of their lives trying to hold hands and run. If the older one runs too fast, the smaller one trips and falls. If she slows down to keep up with the little one, she's only walking. But in the process they never loose that contact of holding tightly to each other's hand. "Come on, Jasmine," Alex encourages patiently. She is walking a little faster and I know is a moment they will be running again. Alex is just waiting for Jasmine to get up a little speed. But as it goes, a one-year old doesn't have a long attention span and as soon as they get up speed she abruptly stops to look at a flower or a bird or just plain change direction and go the other way.

"No, this way," Alex says a little forcefully, and tries to tug Jasmine in the direction they were headed in the first place. Jasmine jerks her hand away and starts to run away form Alex only to be captured and the hand holding starts all over again.

I stand by watching them. Joy, in overwhelming abundance fills my heart as I watch them play. I am fearful of the street with cars whizzing past at the speed of light and of skinned knees and busted lips. I want to run and protect them but they need to learn too. So I stand by and watch with a gentle voice of direction once in a while.

"Alex, honey. Don't pull her too fast, she'll fall."

"Jasmine, don't eat that, baby, it's yucky."

"That's too close to the street guys." And the two of them listen to my instructions and try to obey.

It's like that with God. He looks down at us playing is the sunshine and He beams with pride. We run with each other, holding hands, and we try not to fall as we are whisked along the path of life. Will we experience skinned knees and busted lips? You bet. Do we have more experienced friends and family members encouraging us to "Come on?" Yep. Can we be side tracked? Absolutely! What about the dangers of fast cars and forbidden fruit are we protected? Uh-huh.

God is there with His encouragement and gentle voice of direction.

"You might want to watch what you're putting in your minds with that television."

"Do you think that your brother needs a little pat on the back? He looks sad."

"That man over there looks hungry; maybe he could use some food."

And we try to obey. We grab each other's hands and say, "Come on!"

Pastor appreciation

"Hey, I need some help with…," "But I was hoping you could….," "You don't realize what a trial….," "Do you really think…," (ring, ring, ring, ring,) "But then she said….," "The church isn't any place….," "When do you….," (ring, ring, ring, ring,) "It's time to get ready for…," "Don't forget…," "My little ones are in need….," "I've been waiting for….," (ring, ring, ring, ring,) "Now don't get me wrong….," "How much do I need?" (ring, ring, ring, ring,) "But what about…," "We need to meet…," "People are talking about me….," "Hey, it's your ball game but….," "But he's hurt and needs you to come…," "I'm hoping you will be there…," "Can you do this for me?" "Man, I can't believe he's late again…," (ring, ring, ring, ring,) I wish you would just sit down a minute." "We can't do that…," "It's time to pray…," "Hey, you're way off schedule…," "Fulfill all of your duties…," "The Prayer Chain called…," "He needs you to come…," "Don't forget Zion….," "Can we have a….," "It's time for you to…," "But I thought you would…," (ring, ring, ring, ring, ring, ring,) "We can't make it work without you…," "What I mean is…," "They really need your help…," "I think it's high time you listened…," "It's not your fault but,…" "God said we should…," "I don't want to pry...," "It's not that I don't....," (ring, ring, ring, ring,) "Hey you can't miss this...," "Could I have a minute of your time?"

RING,RING,RING,RING,RING,RING, RING,RING!!!!!!

The urgency with which they feel the call invades their hearts and makes them want to serve and provide and pray for and cry with and counsel and talk to and discipline and love. They are filled with unction. A deep love for God and His people. Tirelessly taking on the battle of lost souls and decaying lives. Hoping they can get the message across to the masses. That no one would be lost. We are covered, from the infant to the elderly. There is a hug and a word of encouragement for every last one of us. Whether we are here or thousands of miles away, the love and concern and prayers are there to help us. We are His children so we are their children. They never complain about the work set before them. They are committed and totally devoted, and for that we thank them.

Tears

She didn't think anyone could see her. She was tired and irritable and wasn't taking any nonsense from anyone. He was bugging her so, she hit him. She knew it was wrong but she lost control. He didn't even cry but the deed was done and it didn't go unseen.

The voice was strong but gentle at the same time. Her name was called and she knew she had been spotted. She stood up and began crying. She took small steps toward the beckoning Giant. Tears flowed down her cheeks as she approached the seat of authority to face her judgment.

The air was thick with the anticipation of what would come next. But, with strong arms, he lifted her up and sat her in his lap. He cradled her in a gentle bear hug. She sobbed on, still waiting for the punishment that she knew she deserved. She was so tired. She had been busy all day and her sniffles were worse and she was hungry and she didn't know where to turn next. Now she was in trouble for being a little girl. Her feelings got away from her and she committed the sin of hitting her brother.

But still he sat and held her. He spoke kindly to her and rocked her. His voice was soft and gentle as he kissed her little head. He admonished her for her deed but he did so with kindness and guidance. He knew that her day had been hectic and that she was tired and that she was sick and that under better circumstances she wouldn't have hit her brother. As he talked and rocked and kissed, her tears began to subside and she melted into his embrace. She was comforted that he loved her in spite of herself. She was relieved. She loved him for loving her and learned a little about forgiveness.

God catches us every day with our hand in the cookie jar and He calls out to us. Sometimes we hear Him and choose to ignore it because we feel we are right about the deed. Other times we argue with Him and try to make Him see our view of things. We try to justify what we've done. That we are tired and hungry and we've had a bad day. And He listens. He knows what kind of day we had. He knows that we seldom think before we act in a time of duress. He is ever patient and kind.

He call's to us in His strong yet gentle voice and how we choose to relate to Him will make the difference. Will we run and hide, or will we stand and argue? Would it be right for us to try to out think God or would it be better for us to face the music? When I'm called, I pray I have the faith of a child. I will go to Him, finger in my mouth, tears coursing down my cheeks, and I'll crawl up into His lap for a hug and a good long cry.

Disease

It's October again and Halloween is just around the corner. Personally, it is the most dreaded month of the year. Great hordes of evil come traipsing through our homes and lives and we have no control unless we want to turn off our televisions, close our eyes and wait for November. It's an evil cancer eating up the imaginations of our children.

But there is another cancer in our lives that is eating away at the church. It is a horrid disease that has early beginnings and has caused grown men to pale and women to simply give up.

This disease has touched us all. Some worse than others and we are all inflicted by it to some degree. Often times we are so caught up in the moment that we don't realize we are feeding it and watching it grow and grow and grow.

We choose not to remember that we are grieving the Holy Spirit who dwells in us and in the church. It has become so dark and so black that it is beginning to blot out the Truth. We do it in the guise of "helping." We take sides in and "pray" for, those who may not want everything known about the concern for which we are praying. This disease is called gossip. Are we really helping each other by making judgments God hasn't made yet?

We are called to love and encourage each other. We are not called to judge, ridicule, lie, cheat and back stab our "family."

Jesus wants us to be in one accord. Bound together by cords that cannot be broken. We need to humble ourselves in the sight of the Lord and He will lift us up.

If we can't bridle our tongues, how will we begin to achieve the holiness we are called to?

"A gossip betrays a confidence, but a trustworthy man keeps a secret."[15]

"A perverse man stirs up dissension, and a gossip separates close friends."[16]

"Without wood a fire goes out; without gossip a quarrel dies down."[17]

November

Thanksgiving

Thanksgiving. What we think of almost automatically is turkey and dressing. Then the real meaning hits and we begin to ponder the things God has done for us. His decision to give His Son, being first and foremost.

This holiday was first celebrated in the United States during early colonial times in New England. In 1621, Governor William Bradford proclaimed a day of thanksgiving and prayer after the harvest. And then in 1623 a drought brought on fasting and prayer which was changed to Thanksgiving because of the rains that came during the prayers. Gradually the custom prevailed in New England of celebrating Thanksgiving after the harvest each year.

In 1817 New York adopted Thanksgiving as an annual custom and by the 19th century many other states joined in. President Lincoln appointed a day of Thanksgiving in 1863 and since then each President has issued a Thanksgiving Day proclamation, generally designating the last Thursday in November as a national holiday.

Thanksgiving is a smell of roasting turkey, dressing and the sweet-tart taste of bright red cranberry sauce. Golden rolls with melting butter and candied yams with little marshmallows baked on top.

As dinner is prepared and the football game blares, children are running through the house playing and enjoying the leaves outside.

When preparations are done, little bowed heads with cold noses and hands listen as the parents and grandparents give thanks to God for all the wonderful bounty He has supplied.

Some day, much quicker than we realize, those little children will be starting traditions of their own and they will be thanking God.

So as the meal is finished and the dishes are done, go kiss the forehead of your sleeping armchair quarter-back and hug those kids, hard, one more time. Then, thank God for His wonderful bounty.

Fast Food

“May I help you?”
"I'd like a large black coffee, a large iced tea with extra ice, and two carrot spice muffins, heated."

"Yes ma'am, that will be $3.83 at the first window."

"Oh, could I please change that black coffee to decaf?"

"Ma'am, you can do anything you want, you have a nice day!"

We were stunned.

"Are we at a drive through?" I asked my husband.

"Maybe they are being robbed and the criminals are nicer than the employees," he said.

We chuckled but it's true. How many times do we go to a fast food restaurant and come out feeling like they did us a favor letting us go in their store and purchase greasy, fat-filled food and enjoy being insulted for dessert? To be treated with courtesy and care was shocking to our systems, especially that early in the morning.

We pulled around to the window and the guy at the register was, check it out, SINGING! He cheerfully took my money and I pulled ahead.

At the next window, the young lady SMILED and handed me my order. Then do you know what she did? She said, get this, "Thank you and have a nice day!"

We laughed. Can you imagine laughing after leaving the Clown's place?

Sometimes churches can be very much like a fast food restaurant. People come to get a quick order of God and a side of Jesus with a large Holy Spirit to go.

How do they perceive us? Are we friendly and willing to help? Or do we send them out into the world with luke-warm feelings of Christian love? Do the people who seek our help receive a decaffeinated version of the true Gospel of Jesus?

I hope the next time someone comes to my church window I have the presence of mind to say, "May I help you? Would you like a hug with that and how about a nice hot prayer to top it off? And by the way, thank you and have a nice day!"

World Series

The World Series was an edge of the seat, stay up late every night and bite your nails kind of time. Every night most of us stayed glued to the television hoping our team would win. There was action packed adventure in every inning and the back and forth daily guess of who would take home the pennant rallied us into a sort of "team" ourselves.

I have never seen so much spitting, scratching, back patting and bat breaking in my life. I thought those guys would drown before they finished playing but it seemed to relax them. I learned more about baseball than before and sort of wished I were at the game. It was sort of a "cat and mouse" situation with the players who wanted to steal bases and the pitcher who had to keep an eye on the base runners as well as throw perfect pitches every time. The outfielders stand way out in the field waiting for the pop flies that will come their way. It kind of makes you wonder if they get stiff waiting to run. Every one working as a unit. A well worked machine. All depending on one another for the plays that will keep the opposition from getting ahead. A ball was hit to left field, a sort of grounder that was saved by a diving catch from Vizquel in what looked like a painful save. He did it. He put forth the extra effort for the team.

We all should work that way. As a well-oiled machine who works in tandem with each other to have a successful team. Every once in awhile going that extra mile. Sometime the Coach will replace us and we will have to give up the ball to someone who can carry on for awhile because we are tired or "off our game." There may be instances where we will need someone to pinch hit for us and then run because we are injured.

Things may come flying at us from left field and we may have to go back to the wall to catch them, saving a run. We might be caught off base, struck out and benched, but we continue the game. We are part of the team. Whether we win or lose, we are in it together. A team. Scratching, spitting, breaking bats, diving, catching, saving and running, together.

The next time your Pitching Coach asks for the ball, realize that it's in the best interest of the team. Not as an affront to you. You may be getting tired and need to sit a spell. But don't spit. The floors get awfully messy that way.

Football

What is it about November that makes things so nostalgic? Is it the smells of dill and cinnamon in the kitchen? How about the football games. Lots of them. Could it be that we remember attending football games in high school? Or perhaps the raking of leaves. We all had to do it as kids. How about the excitement surrounding the hubbub of Holiday time? The air is crisper and we get that rosy hue to our cheeks when we are outside for a while. Cherub cheeks. We had them as children, didn't we?

November is a sleepy time. We are anticipating winter and have worked diligently putting our yards to bed and cleaning furnaces and chimneys and pulling out the long underwear, coats, hats and gloves. My daughter would claim those were indoor necessities at our house. Animals get thicker coats and wild critters are storing up food for their forced incarceration. Sometimes we get a little thicker around the middle too!

It's all in preparation. We are getting ready for the bitter cold of a season where some grumble while they sit in the house watching the ice form and the winds blow. But others of us look at it as an awesome time. Beautiful white snowflakes and crystal tree branches adorn the countryside. A fairyland of hushed enchantment. It takes work to be able to enjoy it. We know its coming and we prepare for its inevitability. We make sure our house is in order.

There is a flurry of activity in Heaven too. Jesus is preparing a place for us. He is ordering all the most beautiful flowers and the finest linens. The utensils are made of gold and the finest crystal glassware is adorning the table. He tries not to think of those who are grumbling and dreading and not preparing. He thinks of those who are excited and who are antici- pating. Those who are thrilled about this awesome time. He is making sure His house is in order. Hey, maybe we'll even get to watch a little football.

Hooray it's November!

The horrible month of October is over. Images of ghosts and gremlins are still in the minds of the children. They think it's all in fun and can only imagine the candy they will get when they go from door to door threatening to do something bad if no candy is dropped into their bags. Our television paves the way for demons and witches to permeate our homes in an unending advertisement of the most dreadful images a human can envision. Grocery and department stores are filled with glaring plastic masks and jack-o-lanterns that leer at you as you try to shop. Little people crane their necks to see all of the ghoulish wear. It's sickening. How do you explain to a three-year old that Halloween is bad? After all, we grew up with it and, well, look at us. Scary isn't it?

But then November comes and the painful celebration of evil comes to a close. At least on the surface. We can go back to teaching our children right from wrong, good from evil, Jesus not Satan. And we hope in the long run they get the picture and decide for themselves that Halloween isn't worth it.

Now we can turn our attention to the forgotten holiday. It's forgotten at least, by the merchants, because let's face it, there are only so many turkeys a person can eat, and well, turkey gift giving just hasn't caught on. Why do I think it's been forgotten? I was in the store the other day and I noticed that the Halloween junk was slowly being moved to the front of the store as it was purchased and the Christmas decorations and clothing were closing in on the very next shelves. No space in between for even a pumpkin pie. It's sad when we are so greedy we can't take time to say, "Thanks."

If Jesus could give thanks, so can we. It would be wonderful if we could take the whole month of November and think of all the things we are thankful for. Stuff like; a free country, food, clothing, a home, friends and family (the real thing not the phone company's version), transportation, a warm bed, children, pets, significant others, a great church, music, comics, blue skies, life, crisp weather, leaves, moms, dads, Jesus, grace, mercy, love, Haagen Dazs, snot nosed kisses, laughter, joy, flowers, golf clubs, and babies to name a few. It would be fun to make a list. And one of the things I'm thankful for besides all that is that it's November. Time for turkey and pumpkin pie. After all, the only good pumpkin is a faceless pumpkin!

Thankfulness

My eyes pop open. My husband is sleeping by my side, the dog at my feet. It takes me a moment to realize what day it is. Oh yeah, Thanksgiving.

"Good morning, Jesus." I whisper.

I get up and stretch as I remember past Thanksgivings with little children around. It won't be that way this year. They have grown and gone to start traditions of their own. They will get up and wash the turkey and cover it with butter and put it in the oven and then starve while its aroma permeates the house.

The bird isn't so big this year and it's easier to handle but I miss the little fingers poking the butter and the small voices asking what each giblet was and what it was used for.

I set the oven for 350 degrees, put the bird in and wash my hands.

"Momma, what does tanksgiving mean?" My memories continue.

I'm sure I told them about the pilgrims and the Mayflower and the Indians, but did I show them Thanksgiving? It was hard when they were little.

I do have so much to be thankful for. Life and love. The gift of Jesus above all. Everything else is just sprinkles on the sundae of life.

In these early morning hours, when the house is still sleeping, God wraps me in His blanket of safety and allows me to regenerate. Prepare for the day, so busy with visits with relatives and the task of watching how much I put in my mouth and what comes out of it. Unsaved members of the family, constantly watching and waiting for the wrong word or something to trip me up on. Yeah, I'm thankful for them too. They keep me on my toes.

The bird smells good. The cat stretches in the sunbeam and meows to go out. The open door reveals crisp autumn air and a beautiful tapestry of leaves. Thank you, Lord.

I shut the door and head for the bedroom.

"Time to get up sleepy head," I whisper to my husband. "It's Thanksgiving! Let us come before him and extol Him with music and song."

December

A Child Is Born

It's an incredible feeling, expecting a grand-child. The bonding that takes place in our hearts grows and grows with each passing month. It could compare to the size of the momma's tummy but, no, it definitely is bigger than that.

I was thinking of the coming Christmas season and what must have been going through the minds of Mary, Joseph and mostly God. If I can love a little baby as much as I already love my grandchild, how much more magnificent God's love must have been for Jesus. The anticipation of Jesus' birth in God's heart would swell in His chest and make His love unfathomable.

His Son, a little baby, soft and pink, would be the greatest gift the world had ever seen.

Oh yes, just like some gifts in today's world, Jesus would not be appreciated. He wouldn't fit. He would be the wrong size or color and He definitely would clash with today's surroundings.

Some would stuff Him under the bed or even try to exchange Him for one who would better serve their purpose. Some just wouldn't "get it," like a punch line of a joke and some would just say, "BAH HUMBUG."

But that little baby came to save the world. He doesn't care if we are filled with sin and are filthy and dirty. He still loves us. With a chest swelling with unfathomable pride and compassion He looks down on us as his little children. Infants and toddlers waiting for *us* this time. Waiting for us to be born into the greatest family.

With expectation of the coming birth, the symbol of Christmas, joy and laughter, love unconditional. Jesus came. A tiny baby, soft and pink.

With a Father's love as a gift to us.

Peace on Earth

Bedtime kisses and shouts of "Good night," come from loud boisterous children. They echo through the night as they scramble off to their beds. They are awaiting Santa and the surprises they will find under the tree in the morning. The evening quiets and parents sit by the fireside and watch the blinking and shimmering of the Christmas tree. Softly playing in the background are strains of *Silent Night, Holy Night*. There is the sound of late night travelers as cars move almost noiselessly through the newly fallen snow.

Christmas is a time when everyone from the poorest to the richest celebrate. Trees with paper chains are just as beautiful as the ones with million dollar decorations. They all mean the same thing. Cheerful holiday music is played in all the stores and on radios. Everyone smiles and feels happy for at least a little while. Rich or poor, young or old, we get together and rejoice in the magnificent gift that was given us.

Several years ago, about two thousand, a child was born on a starlit night, cold and vast. There was no room for His parents as they traveled but they did find shelter in a stable behind an inn. They didn't mind, they had a blessed secret. Through the night a strange peace covered the land and a bright light shone down from the heavens. From far away people saw the star and came to see what had transpired to cause such beauty in the night. Some shepherds were watching their flocks that night and, "and lo, the angel of the Lord came upon them, and the glory of the Lord shone round about them: and they were sore afraid. And the angel said unto them, 'Behold, I bring you good tidings of great joy, which shall be to all people. For unto you is born this day in the city of David a Savior, which is Christ the Lord. And this shall be a sign unto you; ye shall find the babe wrapped in swaddling clothes, lying in a manger.' And suddenly there was with the angel a multitude of the heavenly host praising God, and saying, 'Glory to God in the highest, and on earth peace, good will toward men.'"[18]

From that very night, peace reigned. In the hearts of men and women, spreading the good news. The Christmas promise that was given to us by our Heavenly Father those many years ago that still lives in us today. Shepherds, paupers and kings came to give gifts to the newborn infant who lay in a manger. Serenity surrounded the Holy Family. Even the animals knew. This was the Messiah, the King, the Savior. The Good News was here!

This year as we celebrate Christmas we should remember the REASON. Jesus came, He was born for us. That's why we rejoice. To feel the joy, happiness and comfort our Lord has given us. We are still wise men, we can still seek Him. When you have Jesus in your heart, it's Christmas every day!

Wide Eyed Wonder

The wide-eyed wonder of a child. The first time they see something or someone new and special to them is a beautiful thing. Their little mouths open in awe and amazement of the display before them. It could be the pretty lights decorating a house, a Christmas tree, an overgrown rat named Chuck E. Cheese or Santa Claus. I see that amazement in the faces of my little grandchildren each time something new comes their way.

I took them to Chuck E. Cheeses a couple of months ago to play. Jasmine had never been there before but to Alex it was old stuff. Alex ran off to play as I carried Jasmine into the dining room where all of the animated creatures were singing. I was not expecting the ear-piercing squeal that emoted from her lungs. It was so loud in fact, that all of the people in the restaurant turned to look at her. She had spotted Chuck E. She clapped her hands and wiggled to get down. Once on the floor, she began to dance. Little feet stepping up and down to the music as she twirled around and around, laughing and pointing with excitement. She was so animated herself that the other people were watching her instead of the show. She wanted to be with him every time the curtains opened for him to sing. She would point and laugh and dance with glee.

In contrast, I also took them to see Santa Claus. This time, they didn't laugh or clap their hands. They stood in an awed reverence staring at him. Eyes glued but heads slightly bowed, fingers in their mouths, hanging back waiting. When he spoke they were barely audible in their response. This was Santa after all. The person they had heard about but hadn't seen. They wouldn't sit on his lap but did accept the storybook he offered. And when he said, "Ho Ho Ho", Alex got the strangest look on her face and then smiled. Slightly. It was then that she trusted him enough to sit on his lap but never looked into his face and didn't speak to him.

I wonder which one of those responses I will display when I come face to face with my Jesus. Will I squeal with joy and clap my hands or will I stand in open-mouthed awe at the sight of Him? Will I run to Him and point and dance or will I stand there with my finger in my mouth, head down, hardly daring to speak to Him?

The shepherds and wise men that came to see Him after His birth were filled with awe and reverence. At Christmas time we can renew our spirits, rejoicing in the birth of the Messiah, Jesus. And see Him again, for the first time.

Go To Sleep

"Hush baby, go to sleep."

"But I can't momma, I'm so excited. I can't stand it."

"If you don't go to sleep, morning will never get here."

"Okay, I'll try, but it's Christmas!"

Remember when you were a kid and you would lay awake all night on Christmas Eve and listen for sleigh bells?

Perhaps the sound of reindeer hoofs on the roof? And the whole house would get quiet? Your parents would speak in hushed tomes and hope that you would go to sleep so they could get on with the work of elves. It was a magical time. Your whole world transformed into a fairyland of lights and snow and packages and food. Your eyes would light up at all of the decorations and presents and the homemade candies your mom and grandma would make for the celebration. I remember coconut and chocolate and hand-rolled delectables and my maternal family singing carols while they worked. My father sang *Silent Night* while I tried to nod off to sleep. I will never forget it.

Now I am watching my children teach their children about Christmas. Their bright little eyes taking in every color and special new surprise that is around each corner. They are little and are beginning to learn about the meaning, but right now they are in awe about the changes in their world.

My daughter took her children to see the Christmas lights and they were so excited Jasmine, the two-year old said, "Momma, can I go knock on the doors?" No, honey." My daughter replied. Then Jasmine said, "but momma, I want presents!" Obviously she was a little confused with that other holiday. It's hard for our little ones to keep it all straight. But we teach them and show them about the true meaning of Christmas.

But what about Mary? Don't you suppose she was excited? It was Christmas. Her whole world was changing too. She was far from home, in a stable, and she was with Joseph. He may have been answering her questions.

"Hush Mary, go to sleep."

"But I can't. I'm so excited!"

"But if you try to sleep perhaps it will happen sooner."

And Mary tried to rest as Joseph spoke in hushed tones. The snow falling softly outside the stable doors adding a frosting of decoration to her world. Joseph, singing softly in the silent night while Christmas happened. A beautiful cry of a new born boy. Wrapped in the most precious of swaddling clothes because they were His. The first Christmas. A young girl bringing into the world its first gift. The gift of a Savior.

The Journey

Ladies, imagine being eight to nine months pregnant with all of the uncomfortableness of being huge. You haven't seen your feet in two months. You have to go to the bathroom every five minutes. You feel that your insides are black and blue from all the movement and kicking and then your husband says, "Hey, we have to take a trip."

Gentlemen, your turn. Your beautiful wife is being studied for the new design of the Goodyear Blimp. She waddles when she walks and, well, we won't even talk about her mood swings. You get a message that you have to take her on an unavoidable trip. A long trip. And you get to tell her.

"Joseph!" Can't you make this thing move any faster?"

"No, dear."

"I don't know why we can't just send this information by carrier pigeon. This is ridiculous!"

"Yes, dear."

"My back is hurting and my ankles are swollen!"

"I know, dear."

"When we get to Bethlehem, I'm going to take a long hot bath. I mean it!"

"Yes, dear."

Now gentlemen, you get to tell your wife, "The hotel lost our reservations and there are no rooms, anywhere." Go look into your wife's swollen, grimy face and tell her. Don't want to? Ah, Joseph's job wasn't so easy either was it?

But no matter how difficult, Joseph and Mary were doing God's work. They were to bring forth a child. The Messiah. The One who would save the world. As difficult as the beginning of Jesus' life was for them, imagine the tumultuous experience Mary went through when Jesus laid down His life for us. She didn't understand. She wasn't God. Then elation came. God's promise fulfilled. Radiant and strong, Jesus had emerged from the tomb and gave us the most valuable gift.

Life.

The cost to us? Nothing.

The value? Priceless.

Bibliography

[1] The Bible; Luke 6:38 New International Version
[2] The Bible; 1 Corinthians 13:4-8
[3] Excerpt from *Compton's Interactive Encyclopedia*; Copyright 1993, 1994 Compton's NewMedia. Inc.
[4] The Bible; Isaiah 53:5 New International Version
[5] The Bible; Revelation New International Version
[6] The Bible; Revelation New International Version
[7] The Bible; Matthew 19:21 New International Version
[8] The Bible; Luke 15:20 New International Version
[9] F. Scott Fitzgerald *The Star Spangled Banner*
[10] The Bible; John 8:36
[11] Author Unknown
[12] Author Unknown
[13] The Bible; Titus 2:1
[14] The Bible; Romans 10:15
[15] The Bible; Proverbs 11:13
[16] The Bible; Proverbs 16:28
[17] The Bible; Proverbs 26:20
[18] The Bible; Luke 2:9-14 King James Version

Maggie Mueller grew up in Central Ohio running through the fields of New Albany and attending high school in Westerville. She began writing as a hobby and has completed four books. Maggie and her husband have two children and six grandchildren and they make their home in Columbus.